JOHN MAPSON
(Sunderland)

FORGOTTEN CAPS

1919
1939 - 1946

ENGLAND FOOTBALL INTERNATIONALS OF TWO WORLD WARS

Bryan Horsnell & Douglas Lamming

JOE BACUZZI
Fulham

SPROSTON
SPURS

GEORGE HARKS

LESTER
FINCH

TWO SCHOOLMASTERS
"calling up younger classes
scoaching Britains Reserves"

JACK MARTIN
VILLA & BRUM
C.FWD.—with
F.A HONOURS

TEACHING 'EM
TO SHOOT !

BERNARD JOY
ARSENAL &
ENGLAND
PIVOT

Bernard
shows the
lads how to
keep cool in
a charge

TAKE
KNOCKS &
PLAY
THE
GAME !

ENGLAND WARTIME INTERNATIONALISTS
As seen by artists 'Mac' and Joe Thomas

Published by:
Yore Publications
12 The Furrows, Harefield,
Middx. UB9 6AT.

British Library Cataloguing-in-Publication Data.
A catalogue record for this book
is available from the British Library.

ISBN 1 874427 11 9

Printed and bound by
The Book Factory, London

Contents

INTRODUCTION

The chance acquisition of the programme for the England Vs Wales wartime international at Nottingham Forest's City Ground on 26 April 1941, set me thinking about the England matches and players of the World War Two period, 1939-46.

The goalkeeper for England, in this match against Wales, was Johnny Mapson (Sunderland), who started his Football League career at my local club, Reading. I wondered if this was Mapson's only appearance for England and, indeed, how many other lesser known players represented their country during the war years. Sunderland Supporters Association stalwart, George Forster, put me in touch with the former Reading and Sunderland goalkeeper and I immediately became 'hooked' on finding out all I could about the other wartime internationals.

Since these matches were regarded as 'unofficial', no details are included in Rothmans or other prominent annuals, handbooks or reference books. Geoffrey Green's excellent HISTORY OF THE FOOTBALL ASSOCIATION (published in 1953) gave details of the England line-ups, as did Jack Rollin's SOCCER AT WAR (pub.1985) and Gordon Andrews' DATASPORT BOOK OF WARTIME FOOTBALL 1939-46, but none of them gave detailed information on the matches and the players who took part in them.

Comparison of the information in the aforesaid three publications revealed a number of discrepancies in the actual team line-ups, goalscorers and so on, which made it necessary to consult original newspaper match reports, programmes from the games and also contact a number of the wartime international players themselves. Having unravelled most of the anomalies, my co-author, Douglas Lamming, set-about compiling detailed biographical entries on all the players - as only he can do.

During the course of our research, we identified a number of players who were selected as travelling reserves - but, who didn't actually play - and we felt that these should be included, too. Hence the feature on 'The Nearly Men'.

The inclusion of the World War One details was something of an afterthought, but when we discovered that no international football was played, at all, during the 1914-18 war and only four 'unofficial' England Victory internationals were played in 1919, we felt that it was worthwhile embracing details of these matches and players, to make this as complete a History of England Wartime Internationals as we could.

I was born a few months before the outbreak of World War Two, so by the time I started taking an interest in football - immediately after the war - many of the players included in this book were either dead, retired from the game or coming to the end of their playing careers. It seems appropriate that, at long last, details of these 'Forgotten Caps' should be published to coincide with the 50th Anniversary of V.E. Day.

Since we started this project a number of the players who supplied information or were willing 'interviewees' have passed away, but a least their memories and achievements will be preserved for posterity in the pages of this book.

Bryan Horsnell
April 1995

Co-authors Douglas Lamming (left) and Bryan Horsnell (centre),
with the late Raich Carter - in the Hull City F.C. boardroom

It is hard to realise it is over 55 years since the outbreak of World War 2. Yet things were so different then; for instance, a weekly income of £5 would bring comparative comfort, a mere couple of coppers purchase a copy of the admirable "Topical Times"!

Matters were much different in the football world also. Teams still retained the classical outfield right-back to outside-left positioning although thought-provoking ideas such as the 'W' formation had arrived during the 'Thirties'. The League Cup competitions had not been invented, players' (and managers') incomes, though well above the average, were not the princely sums today's stars can expect.

At the outbreak in September 1939 the Football League programme was three matches old, the Scottish League, which started earlier, five. The authorities acted commendably quickly with regional leagues and war cup competitions soon functioning. Throughout the war years clubs called up professionals in uniform, stationed in their localities. As a result clubs such as Aldershot, centred in a major military base, fielded teams of hitherto unimagined quality. Most of the clubs lost money, especially Wolves whose 1940 balance sheet showed a then considerable £17,717 deficit.

For my own part, I had earlier in 1939 taken an appointment in the Hull area and until called up the following year watched Hull City with their complement of 'own' players and guests perform on the old Anlaby Road ground. The football was reasonably good all things considered, having a natural carefree 'feel' that wasn't present in peacetime's continuous pressure for results. After call-up I saw matches elsewhere when opportunity arose, both in England and during Far East service. They were enjoyed but the return to normality in season 1946/47 was naturally universally welcomed.

Douglas Lamming
April 1995

Dedication

To my Mum and Dad, the late Rose and Ron Horsnell, whose love for the game of football was passed on to me, and to Johnny Mapson (Reading & Sunderland) whose one wartime England international appearance stimulated my interest to undertake this project with Douglas Lamming.

Bryan Horsnell

Acknowledgements

The authors would like to thank the players who have recalled their memories of the wartime internationals, George Forster (Sunderland F.C. Supporters Association), Bryan Hawkins (wartime Wembley Ball-boy) and the following who have provided elusive dates of birth/death, or photo's of some of the more obscure players who represented England in the wartime internationals:-
Chris Bethall, Richard Cohen, Jim Creasy, John D.Cross, Mike Davage, Garth Dykes, Gareth M.Davies, Bob Goodwin, Michael Graham, Ted Green, Malcolm Hartley, Paul Joannou, Richard Lindsay, Brian Mellowship, Andy Porter, Harry Richards, Jim Sims, Cerri Stennett, Dave Sullivan, Mike Swain, Keith Warsop, various Association of Football Statisticians members, and last - but by no means least - Shirley Horsnell for her patient proof reading.

Despite the authors painstaking research, a few of the exact dates of birth/ death and record of the deaths of some of the players, have eluded them. If any of the gaps can be filled in, this additional information would be most welcome.

Publisher's note: Every effort has been made to avoid infringement of copyright of photographs included in this book, although the wide diversity of sources for this material has inevitably led to many examples where the origination is unknown.

THE 'NEARLY' MEN

Before The Football League allowed the use of a substitute - in the case of an injury in 1965 and the F.A. allowing their use in Cup competitions the following season - a team losing a player through injury had to continue the game one man short.

The term 'substitute', in a football context, was unheard of during the period of the first World War and, indeed, during the 1939-46 period, too.

Although reserves were named and had to travel to the matches in which England teams were involved in 1919 and 1939-46, this was arranged purely to cover for any players who had to withdraw due to illness, travelling difficulties, last minute service commitments and so on.

This was illustrated at Cardiff on 11 October 1919, when Birmingham full-back Billy Ball was injured in the first half and took no further part in the game after the interval, England playing the remainder of the game one man short. This situation arose despite Mitchell (Queens Park Rangers) and Edmonds (Watford) being reserves, in attendance at the game.

Several of the players who were named as reserves for these First and Second World War matches eventually gained a place in one of the England international teams, but for others this was the nearest they came to winning an international honour.

The present system of naming 22-men international squads and allowing five - sometimes more - substitutes to be named, increased the chances of any player being selected and actually getting on the field - even just for a few minutes - and gaining an international cap. In order that these players, who were selected as reserves but never actually played in a wartime or Victory international for England, are not forgotten, their biographical details and the match or matches for which they were selected, are detailed under the respective heading of the 'Nearly Men'.

It is interesting to note that Sam Barkas (Manchester City), John Carr (Middlesbrough), Tom Finney and Eric Stephenson (Leeds United), all went on to win 'full' international honours for England, or were already capped before the respective wars.

Key to Who's Who Sections:

Abbreviations:

Apps.	Appearances
cs	Close season
Div.	Division
FA	The Football Association
FL	The Football League
q.v. (quod vide)	a cross reference
sub	Substitute
WW1	First World War
WW2	Second World War

Nomenclature: Clubs are given the title in use when the transfer or other event took place (e.g. Small Heath/Birmingham/Birmingham City refers to a single club). Bradford refers to (defunct) Bradford Park Avenue, while Bradford City is accorded its full title.

Transfer Fees: Many fees quoted are known to be authentic. The remainder are taken from press reports and are considered to be reasonably accurate.

The player's height (feet and inches) and weight (in stones and pounds), where given, follow the year in which these details were provided. A player's nickname or name by which he was more commonly known, is shown in brackets and inverted commas.

WHAT NO CAPS?!

Whilst all the England players who represented their country in peacetime matches were awarded international caps, those who played in the 1919 Victory and 1939-46 wartime and Victory international matches did not receive one of these precious mementos in recognition of their achievements.

Of the 29 different players used in the four 1919 England Victory internationals, 18 had already won 'full' caps prior to the 1914-18 war or went on to win further international honours during their post-war playing careers.

Although the 1919 England Victory international players were not awarded caps, the players who were selected for the two matches against Scotland at Everton and Hampden Park, received a beautiful 9ct. gold medal as a memento of the occasion.

As the same eleven England players took part in both matches, the obverse of the medal has the wording *'The Football Association Victory Internationals England Vs Scotland',* with the England and Scotland flags plus a football in relief.

The reverse of the medal had the wording, *'Goodison Park Liverpool April 26th 1919 - Hampden Park Glasgow May 3rd 1919'*, in relief with the individual player's name engraved.

Although it has not been possible to track one down, it can reasonably be assumed that a similar medal was awarded to each of the England players who took part in the matches against Wales at Cardiff and Stoke in October 1919.

Of the 80 players who represented England in the 1939-46 wartime and Victory internationals - plus the two 1945 'forgotten' internationals against Switzerland - only 42 of these had already won, or went on to win, 'full' international caps.

This was particularly unfortunate for the likes of Joe Bacuzzi who played for England on 13 occasions between 1939 and 1946, but never managed to play in a 'full' international, and therefore never received a coveted 'cap'. However, one of the 'uncapped' England wartime internationalists did, in fact, win a cap after the war. This was Tommy Pearson, Newcastle United's Scotsman, who was called upon as a last minute England replacement, for Eric Brook, in the match against Scotland at St. James Park on 2 December 1939.

But it was a Scottish cap he won, for his appearance for his home country against England in 1947! Pearson also played for Scotland against Belgium in 1947 but, at the time, the Scots only awarded caps to players who played in the Home International Championship matches against England, Wales and Northern Ireland.

Nevertheless, every player who represented England in the wartime and Victory internationals of 1939-46 (including the two 1945 matches in Switzerland) received a beautiful illuminated address, from The

Football Association in April 1946, giving details of all of the matches in which each individual player appeared. In addition the England players who took part in any of the six Victory international matches of 1945-46 were awarded an embroidered blazer badge featuring the England badge and the wording:- *'The Football Association*

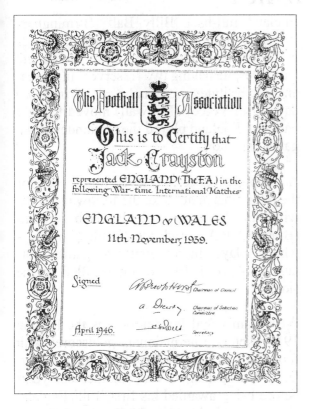

RESERVES

Before The Football League allowed the use of a substitute - in the case of an injury in 1965 and the F.A. allowing their use in Cup competitions the following season - a team losing a player through injury had to continue the game one man short.

The term 'substitute', in a football context, was unheard of during the period of the first World War and, indeed, during the 1939-46 period, too.

Although reserves were named and had to travel to the matches in which England teams were involved in 1919 and 1939-40, this was arranged purely to cover for any players who had to withdraw due to illness, travelling difficulties, last minute service commitments and so on.

This was illustrated at Cardiff on 11 October 1919, when Birmingham full-back Billy Ball was injured in the first half and took no further part in the game after the interval, England playing the remainder of the game one man short. This situation arose despite Mitchell (Queens Park Rangers) and Edmonds (Watford) being reserves, in attendance at the game.

Several of the players who were named as reserves for these First and Second World War matches eventually gained a place in one of the England international teams, but for others this was the nearest they came to winning an international honour.

The present system of naming 22-men international squads and allowing five - sometimes more - substitutes to be named, increased the chances of any player being selected and actually getting on the field - even just for a few minutes - and gaining an international cap.

In order that these players, who were selected as reserves but never actually played in a wartime or Victory international for England, are not forgotten, their biographical details and the match or matches for which they were selected, are detailed below under the heading of the 'Nearly Men'.

It is interesting to note that Sam Barkas (Manchester City), John Carr (Middlesbrough), Tom Finney, Douglas Hunt (Sheffield Wednesday) and Eric Stephenson (Leeds United), all went on to win 'full' international honours for England.

APPEARANCES and GOALSCORERS

WORLD WAR 1

On the outbreak of war in 1914, all international football was suspended - the last pre-war England international being the match at Hampden Park on 4 April 1914.

It was just over five years before an England team was selected again and it's interesting to note that only Sam Hardy (Aston Villa), Joe McCall (Preston) and Joe Smith (Bolton) - who played at Hampden in 1914 - were included in the first of the Victory Internationals, against Scotland, played at Goodison Park, Liverpool on 26 April 1919.

The Football Association used the same eleven players for the return match at Hampden Park the following week, but when the first of the Victory Internationals was played against Wales at Cardiff in October 1919, England fielded a completely different team - with the exception of Syd Puddefoot (West Ham), who retained his place at centre-forward.

England full-back Billy Ball (Birmingham City) was injured in the match against Wales at Cardiff and did not resume in the second half. Despite having two 'reserves' in attendance, substitutes were unheard of in those days. Bill Voicey (Millwall) moved to right back and England played the remainder of the game one short!

A completely different eleven was chosen for the return match at Stoke the following week, with Sam Hardy (Aston Villa), Bob Turnbull (Bradford P.A.), and Joe Smith (Bolton) - who all played in both matches against Scotland in April 1919 - being recalled to the side.

West Ham's Syd Puddefoot was the leading 1919 Victory Internationals goalscorer with four goals in his three appearances for England, but he had to wait another six years before being awarded his first 'full' England cap, against Ireland, on 24 October 1925.

England team v. Scotland
at Goodison Park
Victory International
26 April 1919

(Back row): Mr.A.Warner (Referee), Puddefoot, Longworth, Hardy, Fleetwood, McCall, Grimsdell, J.Elliott (Trainer), Mr.J.Cahill (Linesman)

(Front row): Turnbull, Shea, Duckworth, Smith J., Martin

(Seated): Bagshaw, Gault

VICTORY INTERNATIONALS (1919)

Date	Opponents	Venue	Attend.	Result	1	2	3	4	5	6	7	8	9	10	11
								Season: 1918-19							
26 Apr	SCOTLAND	Everton	45,000	2-2	Hardy	Longworth	Duckworth (c)	Fleetwood	McCall	Grimsdell	Turnbull (1)	Shea	Puddefoot (1)	Smith J. *	Martin
3 May	SCOTLAND	Hampden	80,000	4-3	Hardy	Longworth	Duckworth (c)	Fleetwood	McCall	Grimsdell (2)	Turnbull	Shea	Puddefoot (2)	Smith J. *	Martin
								Season: 1919-20							
11 Oct	WALES	Cardiff	20,000	1-2	Williamson	Ball	A.E.Knight (c)	Voisey	Hilditch	Grenyer	E.H.Hendren	Buchan	Puddefoot (1)	Barnes H.	Brooks
18 Oct	WALES	Stoke	16,000	2-0	Hardy	Smith J.#	Hudspeth (c)	Bagshaw	Parker	Watson	Turnbull	Whittingham(1)	Cock	Smith J.(1) *	Hodkinson

(c) denotes Captain. * Bolton player. # West Bromwich Albion player. (Where first name initials are given before a surname, this indicates an Amateur player)

The England team
that met Wales
in Cardiff
11 October 1919:

(Players in kit only)

(Back row) Ball, Williamson,
Grenyer, Voisey.
(Middle row) Brooks, Buchan,
A.E.Knight (capt.), Barnes,
Hendren.
(Front row) Puddefoot,
Hilditch.

1919 England Victory Internationals Summary:

	Home						Away					
	Pl.	W.	D.	L.	F.	A.	Pl.	W.	D.	L.	F.	A.
Vs. Scotland	2	0	1	0	2	2	1	0	0	4	3
Vs. Wales	2	1	0	0	2	0	2	1	0	1	2
Totals:	4	1	1	0	4	2	1	0	1	5	5

BAGSHAW, J(ohn) James
(Derby County)

(1 app. for England in a 1919 'Victory' international)
Born: Derby, 25 Dec. 1885
Died: 25 Aug. 1966
1919: 5-9, 11-10

Career: Fletcher's Athletic (Derby works team); Graham Street Primitives (Derby); Derby County Oct. 1906; Notts County Feb. 1920 after being a guest player 1918/19; Watford May 1921 for a brief spell, subsequently assisting Ilkeston United and Grantham. During WW2 scouted for both Nottingham clubs and Coventry City besides working on Forest's training staff.

Other Honours: England (1 'full' app.)
(Derby Co.) FL Div.2 champions 1912, 1915

Right-half, sometimes centre-half. A player both hardy and perceptive, a fine servant for Derby County over a long period. Accurate in distribution, Bagshaw also tackled well, aided by the capacity to move quickly. He was employed by Raleigh Industries after retiring from playing.

BALL, William
(Birmingham)

(1 app. for England in a 1919 'Victory' international)
Born: Dudley, Worcs. 9 April 1886
Died: 30 Sep. 1942
1919: 5-8, 11-7

Career: Dudley Welfare; Stourbridge; Leamington; Wellington Town; Birmingham May 1911; Cannock Town Oct. 1921 and had another spell with Wellington Town before retiring in 1924.

Right-back. Stocky competitive defender with a then unfashionable attacking bent. Partnered the long-serving Frank Womack during his decade as a St. Andrews notable. This decade, of course, took in the whole of the Great War period so his League and FA Cup appearances totalled a relatively modest 165. Ball was on Brum's books in 1920/21 when the club headed the Division 2 table, but was no longer a first team choice and thus did not qualify for a championship medal.

BARNES, Horace
(Manchester City)

(1 app. for England in a 1919 'Victory' international)
Born: Wadsley Bridge, Sheffield, 3 Jan. 1890
Died: 12 Sep. 1961
1913: 5-7½, 11-4

Career: Birley Carr (Sheffield Sunday School League); Derby County Oct. 1908; Manchester City May 1914 (£2500, the highest authenticated fee at the time); Preston North End Nov. 1924 (£2750); Oldham Athletic Nov. 1925 (£1250); Ashton National Aug. 1927 - cs 1931.

Other Honours: Football League (2 apps.)
(Derby Co.) FL Div.2 champions 1912

Born: Brierley Hill, Staffs. 28 Mar. 1890
Died: 13 Jan. 1960
1921: 5-2, 9-0
Career: Brierley Hill Alliance; Bilston United; Cradley Heath St. Luke's; Wolverhampton Wanderers amateur before signing prof Aug. 1910; Tottenham Hotspur July 1922; Kidderminster Harriers cs 1924; Southend United Jan. 1925; Kidderminster Harriers again June 1925, later assisting Cradley Heath and Stourbridge before retiring in 1927.

Other Honours: Football League (1 app.)
(Wolves) FA Cup finalist 1921

Outside-left. They never came smaller than Sammy Brooks who was even shorter (and a stone lighter) than the celebrated "Fanny" Walden. He had a fine run with Wolves, his trickery and elusiveness compensating for lack of height and weight, establishing himself as their regular left-winger in 1912. His peacetime League record for the Molyneux club was 217 appearances, 51 goals. In 1921/22 two of his brothers were also on Wolves' books.

Inside-left. Turned out to be a durable performer - in the Football League until aged 37 and was still playing Cheshire County League football in his 41st year. Barnes, an immediate success with Derby, was bustling and brave and packed a fierce left-foot shot. A consistent scorer throughout his long career, his total FL figures read 450 appearances, 226 goals.

BUCHAN, Charles Murray
(Sunderland)

(1 app. for England in a 1919 'Victory' international)
Born: Plumstead, London, 22 Sep. 1891
Died: 25 June 1960
1921: 6-1, 12-1
Career: Woolwich schools and junior football; Woolwich Polytechnic (Woolwich Arsenal amateur Dec. 1908); Northfleet Nov. 1909; Leyton as a prof Mar. 1910; Sunderland Mar. 1911 (£1250); Arsenal July 1925 (£4100, boosted by £100 paid to Sunderland for every goal scored by Buchan during his first Arsenal season); retired May 1928.

BROOKS, Samuel Ernest
(Wolverhampton Wanderers)

(1 app. for England in a 1919 'Victory' international)

Other Honours: England (6 'full' apps.)
Football League (10 apps.)
(Sunderland) FL champions 1913
FA Cup finalist 1913
(Arsenal) FA Cup finalist 1927

Inside-right, occasionally centre-forward. One of the early twentieth century's greatest names, a subtle performer master of all the inside-forward arts. His modest haul of caps, considered by many as scandalous, was attributed to the inability of less gifted colleagues to respond to these subtleties. Charlie went into sports journalism with the "Daily News" (later the "News-Chronicle"), writing on soccer and golf. He became first editor of "Football Monthly" on the magazine's launch in 1951 and a football commentator on BBC radio. A useful cricketer, he assisted Durham CCC in the Minor Counties soon after WW1.

COCK, John Gilbert
(Huddersfield Town)
(1 app. for England in a 1919 'Victory' international)
Born: Hayle, Cornwall, 14 Nov. 1893
Died: 19 Apr. 1966
1914: 5-10, 11-6
Career: West Kensington United; Forest Gate; Old Kingstonians Dec. 1912 (Brentford amateur Mar. 1914); Huddersfield Town Apr. 1914; Cheslea Oct. 1919 (£2650); Everton Jan. 1923; Plymouth Argyle Mar. 1925; Millwall Athletic Nov. 1927 (£2000); Folkestone Jul. 1931; Walton & Hersham Mar. 1932. Millwall manager Nov. 1944 - Aug. 1948.

Other Honours: England (2 'full' apps.)
Football League (2 apps.)
(Millwall) FL Div.3 (South) champions 1928

Centre-forward. A great name of the 'twenties, successful with all his League clubs - athletic, possessing all round skills, and a regular scorer. Well known as the best dressed footballer of his day, Jack had connections with the film and stage world, and had a fine tenor voice. His wartime Army record was meritorious, rising to the rank of Sgt.major and winning both the DCM and MM. A New Cross licensee latterly. Jack's brother, Donald also a centre-forward, was a member of the Notts County's 1923 Second Division championship side.

DUCKWORTH, Fred
(Blackburn Rovers)
(2 apps. for England in 1919 'Victory' internationals)
Born: Blackburn, 1892
1919: 5-6½, 10-7
Career: Played in local Blackburn sides - in succession for Futhergate School, Bastwell Etrurians, St. Stephen's, Blackburn Trinity and Blackburn YMCA - before joining Blackburn Rovers in Jan. 1910. Retired through injury June 1922.

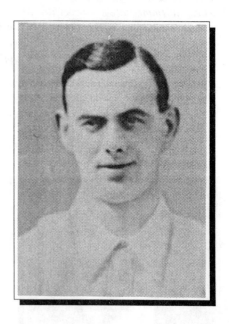

Left-back. Did not make Rover's League team until the first post-war season, that is after two England 'Victory' international selections, due to the renowned Crompton/Cowell partnership. However, Duckworth had built a reputation with fine displays in the Central League side, showing versatility by appearing also at half-back and outside-right. Settled at left-back in Cowell's wartime absence when, despite a slight build, his quickness, bravery and accurate clearances from all angles were appreciated.

A plumber by trade and a part-time professional, Fred's retirement came from an unusual injury. In an East Lancs Charity Cup-tie in Apr. 1921 he broke his left forearm in two places and the bone would not re-set properly.

FLEETWOOD, Thomas
(Everton)
(2 apps. for England in 1919 'Victory' internationals)
Born: Toxteth Park, Liverpool, 6 Dec. 1888
1919: 5-9, 12-0
Career: Hindley Central; Rochdale Oct. 1908; Everton Mar. 1911 (£460); Oldham Athletic Aug. 1923 (£750); Chester Sep. 1924

Other Honours: Football League (5 apps.)
(Everton) FL champions 1915

Right-half and sometimes centre-half with the capability of also playing full-back and inside-forward. Variously described at different times as "strong and determined" and "versatile and willing". When a child moved from Liverpool to Bolton where prominence in Sunday schools football led to an unsuccessful trial with Bolton Wanderers. Turned professional with Hindley Central, scoring 28 goals one season for Rochdale and became a recognised half-back during his dozen years at Goodison. Tom, appointed skipper on arriving at Oldham, suffered a bad injury on his debut and consequently played little for that club.

GRENYER, Alan
(Everton)
(1 app. for England in a 1919 'Victory' international)
Born: North Shields, Northumberland, 31 Aug. 1892
Died: June 1953
1919: 6-0, 12-7
Career: Collingwood; North Shields FC; North Shields Athletic; Everton Nov. 1910; South Shields Nov. 1924-1929.

Other Honours: Football League (1 app.)
(Everton) FL champions 1915

Left-half. Shared the left-half spot at Goodison from 1912 to 1915 with Harry Makepeace, the famous 'double international' (ie. he had represented England at both soccer and cricket). Both players made sufficient appearances in 1914/15 to qualify for a League championship medal. Grenyer had been a forward originally but was a left-half for the whole of his senior career. He was expert at heading the ball and also noted for judicious and accurate distribution.

GRIMSDELL, Arthur
(Tottenham Hotspur)
(2 apps. for England in 1919 'Victory' internationals)
Born: Watford, 23 Mar. 1894
Died: 12 Mar. 1963
1919: 5-11, 12-7

Career: Watford Schools; Watford St. Stephen's; Watford FC amateur 1909, turning prof Nov. 1911; Tottenham Hotspur Mar. 1912 (£350); Clapton Orient as player/sec-manager May 1929; Was a Watford FC director 1945-51.

Other Honours: England (6 'full' apps.)
Football League (1 app.)
(Spurs) FL Div. 2 champions 1920
FA Cup winner 1921

Left-half. One of the greatest players ever to fill the position and an inspiring skipper. Dominating, aggressive and naturally unorthodox, Arthur was really a sixth forward, his aggression well illustrated in Spurs' 1920 promotion campaign. He then netted 14 goals, a record for a midfield player that stood until 1952. A Watford sports outfitter and brother of the amateur international, E.F. Grimsdell, he played Minor Counties cricket for Hertfordshire as a wicket-keeper/batsman from 1922 to 1947.

HARDY, Sam
(Aston Villa)
(3 apps. for England in 1919 'Victory' internationals)
Born: Newbold, Chesterfield, 26 Aug. 1883
Died: 24th Oct. 1966
1919: 5-9¼, 12-0
Career: Newbold White Star; Chesterfield Town Apr. 1903; Liverpool Oct. 1905 (£500); Aston Villa May 1912; Nottingham Forest Aug. 1921; retired cs 1925.

Other Honours: England (21 'full' apps.)
Football League (10 apps.)
(Liverpool) FL champions 1906
(Villa) FA Cup winner 1913, 1920
(Forest) FL Div.2 champions 1922

Goalkeeper adjudged the finest of his day and among the finest of all time. Sam's unspectacular mien actually highlighted marvellous anticipation that made a taxing job look easy. One third of the celebrated Hardy-Crompton-Pennington England defence, he won top honours with three League clubs over a 16-year period. As a veteran of 39 he conceded but 23 goals in 32 League games in Forest's 1921/2 championship campaign. Served in the Navy during WW1 and was latterly a Chesterfield licensee.

HENDREN, Elias Henry ("Patsy")
(Brentford)
(1 app. for England in 1919 'Victory' international)
Born: Turnham Green, Middlesex, 5 Feb. 1889
Died: 4 Oct. 1962
1923: 5-7, 12-6
Career: Junior football to Brentford c.1907; Manchester City Mar. 1908; Coventry City Oct. 1909; Brentford again Aug. 1911; retired cs 1927.

Other Honour: Southern League (1 app.)

Outside-left, occasionally outside-right. Thickset winger possessing speed and the capacity to place his centres with consummate accuracy. More famous, of course, as the great Middlesex and England right-hand batsman, assisting his county 1907-37 (581 matches), and England in 51 Tests. His batting feats included hitting over 3000 runs in a season three times. His highest single innings was 301 not out against Worcestershire in 1933.

Centre- or wing-half. Typical comments by soccer writers during Clarrie's playing career were "a rare spoiler", and, "a stopper and wholesaler provider of opportunities". Certainly his defensive qualities were notable but the second quote's mention of creative skills makes it the more rounded picture. For good distribution and eye for position were in evidence too. Post-WW2 he was for a time Witton Albion's team secretary, leaving the post during season 1966/67.

HODKINSON, Joseph
(Blackburn Rovers)
(1 app. for England in a 1919 'Victory' international)
Born: Lancaster, 1889
Died: 18 June 1954
1919: 5-8, 11-0
Career: Lancaster St. Mary's; Lancaster Town; Glossop cs 1909; Blackburn Rovers Jan. 1913 (£1000); Lancaster Town again Apr. 1923; retired Jan. 1925.

Other Honours: England (3 'full' apps.)
Football League (2 apps.)
(Blackburn Rovers) FL champions 1914

HILDITCH, Clarence George ("Lal")
(Manchester United)
(1 app. for England in a 1919 'Victory' international)
Born: Hartford, Cheshire, 2 June 1894
1922: 5-10, 11-0
Career: From his local side (Hartford FC) went on to assist well known Cheshire non-League clubs - in succession Northwich Victoria, Witton Albion and Altrincham - before becoming a Manchester United amateur in Jan. 1916, turning prof in 1919. Acted as United's player/manager Oct. 1926 - Mar. 1927 between one manager's suspension and another taking over. Retired cs 1932.

Other Honour: Member of FA touring party to South Africa 1920

Outside-left. Especially regarded for pinpoint accuracy when middling the ball and great pace. The fact he was innately an individualist did not detract from making a full contribution to team work. After retiring, became - in the late 1920's - a licensee in his native Lancaster.

HUDSPETH, Francis Carr
(Newcastle United)

(1 app. for England in a 1919 'Victory' international)
Born: Percy Main, Northumberland, 20 Apr. 1890
Died: 8 Feb. 1963
1922: 5-8, 11-7
Career: Scotswood; Newburn; Clare Vale; North Shields Athletic; Newcastle United Mar. 1910 (£100); Stockport County Jan. 1929; Crook Town Dec. 1930. Rochdale trainer July 1933; Burnley assistant trainer 1934-45, when he left football.

Other Honours: England (1 'full' app.)
(Newcastle Utd) FL champions 1927
FA Cup winner 1924

Left-back. A great Newcastle servant reliable in all aspects of his craft, at the outset partner of the legendary Bill McCracken. Besides the unusual length of his St. James Park service, Frank was reckoned, at 35½ years of age, the oldest England debutante up to Leslie Compton's 1950/51 debut. Appeared in peacetime 430 League and 42 FA Cup matches for Newcastle and captained the side in both the 'twenties championship and FA Cup-winning triumphs.

KNIGHT, Arthur Egerton
(Portsmouth)

(1 app. for England in a 1919 'Victory' international)
Born: Godalming, Surrey, 7 Sep. 1887
Died: 10 Mar. 1956
1919: 5-11, 12-0
Career: King Edward VI Grammar School (Guildford) and junior football; Portsmouth 1909-22; Corinthians 1921-31.

Other Honours: England (1 'full' app.)
England amateur international (30 apps.)
(Portsmouth) Southern League champions 1920

Left-back. A gifted amateur with footballing longevity, playing top grade amateur soccer when well past 40. A doughty tackler and good at heading, Knight's positional sense compensated for a certain lack of pace. He was also a useful cricketer, making several appearances for Hampshire in the period 1913-23. Served in the Army during the first World War, rising to the rank of captain.

LONGWORTH, Ephraim
(Liverpool)

(2 apps. for England in 1919 'Victory' internationals)
Born: Halliwell, Bolton, 2 Oct. 1887
Died: 7 Jan. 1968
1919: 5-8, 11-0
Career: Bolton Schools; Bolton St. Luke's; Hyde St. George's as a prof; Bolton Wanderers June 1907 following brief spells with Halliwell Rovers and Hyde; Leyton late in 1908; Liverpool May 1910; retired cs 1928, subsequently serving on the club's training staff.

Other Honours: England (5 'full' apps.)
Football League (6 apps.)
(Liverpool) FL champions 1922, 1923
FA Cup finalist 1914
Member of FA touring party to South Africa 1920

Right-back. His bowed legs, like Joe Mercer's in a later era, were much caricatured.

More seriously, Longworth used those legs equally well, the clearances usually finding the team-mate to whom directed. Very sound tactically also and the first Liverpool player to captain England. Contemporaries usually shortened his biblical first name to Eph. Played his final First Division game on Apr. 21, 1928, when well over 40 years of age.

MARTIN, Henry
(Sunderland)
(2 apps. for England in 1919 'Victory' internationals)
Born: Selston, Notts., 5 Dec. 1891
1919: 5-10, 12-0
Career: Sutton Junction 1909; Sunderland Jan. 1912; Nottingham Forest May 1922; Rochdale June 1925 - cs 1929 when he was appointed that club's trainer (1 FL appearance 1930/31); Mansfield Town manager Dec. 1933 - Mar. 1935; Swindon Town trainer cs 1936 to the mid-1950's.

Other Honours: England (1 'full' app.)
Football League (3 apps.)
(Sunderland) FL champions 1913
FA Cup finalist 1913

McCALL, Joseph
(Preston North End)
(2 apps. for England in 1919 'Victory' internationals)
Born: Kirkham, Lancs., 6 July 1886
Died: 3 Feb. 1965
1919: 5-8½, 11-12
Career: Kirkham FC; Preston North End on amateur forms during season 1905/06, turning prof July 1906; retired May 1925.

Other Honours: England (5 'full' apps.)
Football League (2 apps.)
(PNE) FL Div.2 champions 1913
FA Cup finalist 1922

Centre-half. Must be classified among the game's leading pivots. Joe, although of attacking inclination, never seemed out of position, fed his wingmen with long raking passes and was stylish withal. Played cricket professionally too - for Lancashire clubs, and was cricket coach to Stonyhurst College, the public school. Obviously a busy man for he was also a smallholder and poultry farmer at Wrea Green near Kirkham.

Outside-left, unusually big for a winger so consequently that much more difficult to contain. Harry also possessed a raking stride and the ability to middle the ball accurately when travelling at speed. Capped for England early in his senior career, he made his final League appearance when aged 40. His 1922 transference was actually a renewed acquaintance with Forest for he had been a wartime guest at Trent Bridge. Had a notably long stint as a Swindon Trainer, which lasted around two decades.

PARKER, Charles William
(Stoke)

(1 app. for England in a 1919 'Victory' international)
Born: Seaham Harbour, Co. Durham, 21 Sep. 1891
1919: 5-9, 11-4
Career: Seaham Albion; Seaham Harbour (North-Eastern League); Stoke 1914; Sunderland Sep. 1920 (£3,300); Carlisle United May 1929; Chopwell Institute cs 1930.

Other Honours: Football League (1 app.)
(Stoke) Southern League Div.2 champions 1915

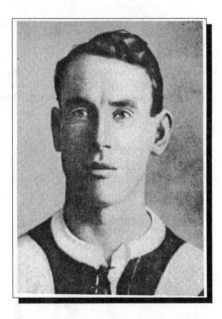

Centre-half. Cost Sunderland a fat fee by early post-war standards but it seemed his first team place would be lost when another pivot, Michael Gilhooley, joined for a record £5,250. But the latter was quickly sidelined by serious injury and Charlie's capable all-round displays continued in a senior setting. With wing-halves Willie Clunas and Arthur Andrews he formed an intermediate line that held sway at Roker Park from 1923 to 1927, and which performed consistently well. He was unaffected by the lack of physical advantages most centre-halves enjoy.

PUDDEFOOT, Sydney Charles
(West Ham United)

(3 apps. for England in 1919 'Victory' internationals)
Born: Limehouse, London, 17 Oct. 1894
Died: 2 Oct. 1972
1919: 5-10, 12-7
Career: East London schools football; Conder Athletic; Limehouse Town; West Ham United on amateur forms during season 1912/13, turning prof. the following season; Falkirk February 1922 (for a then record £5,000); Blackburn Rovers Feb. 1925 (£4,000); West Ham United again Feb. 1932; retired cs 1933. Coach in Turkey with Fenerbahce, Istanbul 1933/34 and Galatia Suray 1934/35; Northampton Town manager Mar. 1935 - Mar. 1937; returned to Turkey later in 1937, coaching in Istanbul until 1940. In the 1960's had a spell scouting for Southend United.

Other Honours: England (2 'full' apps.)
Football League (2 apps.)
Southern League (1 app.)
(Blackburn) FA Cup winner 1928

Inside-right/centre-forward. A natural ball player and, although unorthodox, an excellent team man bringing colleagues into action with telling passes. Earned a big reputation early because of his several scoring feats. Surprised many on joining a Scottish club in 1922, but 'Puddy' had been a guest player for Falkirk during the 1914/18 war. Worked as a Civil Servant after leaving football. He was a good cricketer, playing on 8 occasions for Essex in 1922/23.

SHEA, Daniel
(Blackburn Rovers)

(2 apps. for England in 1919 'Victory' internationals)
Born: Wapping, East London, 6 Nov. 1887
Died: 25 Dec. 1960
1919: 5-6, 10-4
Career: Pearl United; Manor Park Albion; West Ham United Nov. 1907, originally as an amateur; Blackburn Rovers Jan. 1913 (for a then record £2,000 of which the player received £550); West Ham United again May 1920 (£1,000); Fulham Nov. 1920; Coventry City cs 1923; Clapton Orient Mar. 1925; Sheppey United Oct. 1926.

Other Honours: England (2 'full' apps.)
Football League (2 apps.)
Southern League (3 apps.)
(Blackburn) FL champions 1914

Inside-right. Prominent before and after the Great War, a subtle performer with magnificent ball control and delicate dribbling skills. Could shoot suddenly and hard too, and scored consistently. Employed in a shipping office before taking up football professionally and as a dock worker afterwards. In the 'thirties ran a West Ham sub-Post Office. Of Irish parentage.

SMITH, Joseph
(Bolton Wanderers)

(3 apps. for England in 1919 'Victory' internationals)
Born: Dudley Port, Staffs., 25 June 1889
Died: 11 Aug. 1971
1922: 5-7¼, 12-8
Career: Newcastle Parish Schools Association (N. Staffs. Sunday Schools League); Bolton Wanderers May 1908; Stockport County

Mar. 1927 (around £1,000); Darwen cs 1929; Manchester Central June 1930; Hyde United Sep. 1930; Reading manager July 1931 - Aug. 1935. Blackpool manager until retiring in Apr. 1958.

Other Honours: England (5 'full' apps.)
(Bolton) FA Cup winner 1923, 1926.
Member of FA touring party to South Africa 1920

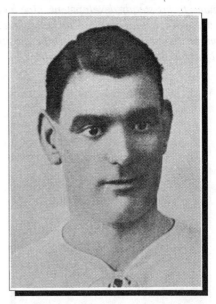

Inside-left. Could also play centre-forward. Twice captained Bolton to Wembley Cup triumphs and formed a famous left-wing with Welsh cap, Ted Vizard, that lasted an extraordinarily long time, from 1910 to 1927. Joe was a thrusting, assertive attacker who packed a thunderbolt shot. He scored regularly, his Wanderers' figures reading 277 in 492 FL and FA Cup outings. In season 1920/21 his 38 goals equalled the then League record. His jocular and easy going managerial style proved extremely effective. In 4 seasons with Reading the club never finished lower than 4th, while Blackpool enjoyed their richest and most successful period during his long stint at Bloom-field Road.

SMITH, Joseph
(West Bromwich Albion)

(1 app. for England in a 1919 'Victory' international)
Born: Darby End nr. Dudley, Worcs., 10 Apr. 1890
Died: 9 June 1956
1922: 5-7, 11-0
Career: Netherton St. Andrew's; Darby End Victoria; Cradley Heath St. Luke's; West Bromwich Albion May 1910; Birmingham May 1926; Worcester City as player/manager May 1929 - 1932.

Other Honours: England (2 'full' apps.)
(WBA) FL champions 1920
FL Div.2 champions 1911

Right-back. First choice right-back at The Hawthorns from joining until his departure 16 years later - ample evidence of quite outstanding consistency. For all but 4 of the peacetime seasons (plus 1914/15, which was played on a peacetime basis) he partnered the legendary Jesse Pennington, a happening that doubtless contributed to his steady development. Joe had most of the defensive virtues - sound tackling, intelligent distribution and so on - and thoughtful positioning masked the fact he was no speed merchant.

TURNBULL, Robert Joseph
(Bradford)
(3 apps. for England in 1919 'Victory' internationals)
Born: South Bank, Middlesbrough, 17 Dec. 1895
Died: 18 Mar. 1952
1922: 5-7½, 12-3
Career: South Bank Schools; South Bank East End; Army football; Bradford (Park Avenue) Jan. 1918; Leeds United May 1925; Rhyl Athletic Sep. 1932; retired 1933.

Other Honours: England (1 'full') app.
Member of FA touring parties to South Africa 1920 and 1929

Outside-right. One of the great talents to emerge from the 1914/18 War period, sensationally scoring 5 goals on his senior debut for Park Avenue on New Year's Day 1918, playing inside-left. As a wingman at his best, Bob was fast, showing clever footwork and accuracy in passing. No mean goalscorer for an outside-right either, notching 95 in an aggregate 438 FL and FA Cup appearances for his two League clubs. A steelworker both before and after his football career.

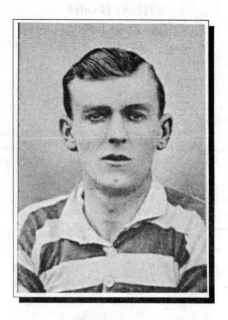

VOISEY, William ("Banger")
(Millwall Athletic)
(1 app. for England in 1919 'Victory' international)
Born: Isle of Dogs, Millwall, 19 Nov. 1891
Died: 19 Oct. 1964
1919: 5-7, 11-0
Career: Millwall schools football afterwards assisting local clubs, Glengall Rovers and St. John's, before joining Millwall Athletic on amateur forms during season 1908/09, prof. 1909/10; Bournemouth & Boscombe Athletic June 1923; retired cs 1924. Leytonstone trainer/coach 1924; Fulham assistant trainer 1930, trainer 1934; Millwall trainer June 1939 - 1949 (acting team manager during WW2, 1940 - Nov. 1944), subsequently serving the club as chief scout. Retired 1962.

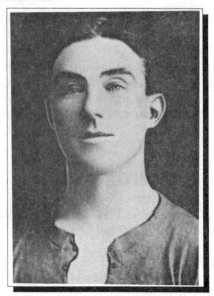

Right-half. An outstanding servant to Millwall, his total length of service, in several different roles, adding up to some 38 years. As a player he was known as a tenacious wing-half of attacking bent, wont to employ a rocket shot (hence the nickname 'Banger'). Had a great Army record in WW1 rising to the rank of Btn. Sgt.Major and being awarded the DSM, MM and Belgian Croix de Guerre.

WATSON, William

(Burnley)

(1 app. for England in a 1919 'Victory' international)
Born: Birkdale, Southport, 11 Sep. 1890
Died: 1 Sep. 1955
1919: 5-8, 11-8
Career: Southport schoolboy football; Blowick Wesleyans; Southport Central 1907, turning prof. 1908; Burnley Mar. 1909 (£200); Accrington Stanley player/coach cs 1925; Blackburn Rovers coach for a time when he also captained their 'A' team.

Other Honours: England (3 'full' apps.)
Football League (5 apps.)
(Burnley) FL champions 1921
FA Cup winner 1914

Left-half. In December 1922 the "Lancashire Daily Post" critic listed Watson's talents, finishing by saying he had the edge over contemporaries Grimsdell, Bromilow et al (high praise indeed!).

True or not, Watson had polish, skill, consistency and all round competence in plenty without being showy in any degree. After leaving the game first worked as an ironmonger and later as a decorator. Twice served terms as a Southport borough councillor.

WITTINGHAM, Robert

(Chelsea)

(1 app. for England in a 1919 'Victory' international)
Born: Goldenhill, Stoke-on-Trent, 1889
Died: June 1926
1919: 5-9, 12-4
Career: Goldenhill FC; Crewe Alexandra; Blackpool cs 1907; Bradford City Jan. 1909; Chelsea Apr. 1910 (£1,300); Stoke Oct. 1919; retired on health grounds cs 1920, unsuccessfully attempting a comeback with Wrexham in Nov. 1922.

Other Honour: Football League (1 app.)

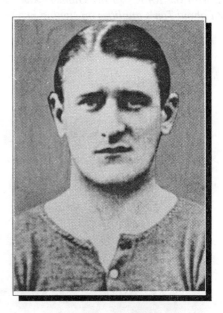

Centre-forward/inside-right. Notability from the immediate pre-1914 period. Scored heavily then with all three of his League sides, aggregating 139 goals in 231 FL and FA Cup outings. Most difficult for opposing defenders to counter with his powerful physique and explosive shooting from any and every angle. He established a new seasonal League record for Chelsea (30 goals in 1910/11). Bob died tragically early, aged only 37, from tuberculosis.

WILLIAMSON, Ernest Clarke ("Tim")
(Arsenal)

(1 app. for England in a 1919 'Victory' international)
Born: Murton Colliery, Co. Durham, 24 May 1890
Died: 30 Apr. 1964
1919: 5-9, 12-3
Career: Murton Red Star; Wingate Albion; Croydon Common June 1913; Arsenal Apr. 1919 (£150); Norwich City June 1923; retired 1925

Other Honour: England (2 'full' apps.)

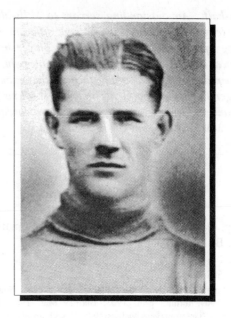

Goalkeeper. A confident performer and an agile one whose confidence transferred itself to fellow defenders. Is thought to have acquired his nickname from an older namesake, the great Middlesbrough and England custodian, R.G. ("Tim") Williamson. From the mid-'twenties a Norwich licensee for many years and also for a time a bowling club's groundsman. A guest player for Arsenal during the 1914/18 War while serving with the RASC, so the Gunners knew at first hand all about Tim's qualities on signing him in 1919.

CARR, John

(Middlesbrough)

Born: South Bank, Middlesbrough, 26 Nov. 1892
Died: 10 May 1942
1919: 5-8½, 11-8

Career: South Bank schools and junior football; South Bank FC; Middlesbrough Jan. 1911; Blackpool May 1930 (£500); Hartlepools United player/coach July 1931, manager Apr. 1932 - Apr. 1935; Tranmere Rovers manager May 1935 - Nov. 1936; Darlington manager Oct. 1938 to his death.

Other Honours: England (2 'full' apps.)
Football League (3 apps.)
(South Bank) FA Amateur Cup finalist 1910
(Middlesbrough) FL Div.2 champions 1927, 1929
(England reserve Vs. Wales 18 Oct. 1919)

Outside-right/inside-forward. The most prominent of three brothers who gave Middlesbrough fine service over two decades, 1910-1930 (there was also a fourth brother who appeared three times in Boro's League side during season 1910/11, an amateur). Jackie was versatile and a craftsman, his subtle skills contributing in no small way to the scoring feats of Middlesbrough forwards such as Elliott, Pease and Camsell.

EDMONDS, George William Neville

(Watford)

Born: Finsbury, London, 4 Apr. 1893
Died: 10 Dec. 1989
1919: 5-7, 12-4

Career: With two Herts. Junior sides, St. Stephen's and Andras FC, before joining St. Alban's City in 1910; Watford on amateur forms 1912, turning professional cs 1914; Wolverhampton Wanderers May 1920 (£3,000 including another player); Fulham Oct. 1923; Watford again Aug. 1926; retired cs 1927.

Other Honours: (Watford) Southern League champions 1915
(Wolves) FA Cup finalist 1921
(England reserve Vs. Wales 11 Oct. 1919)

Centre-forward. As a boy had played in the same school team as the great Spurs and England wing-half, Arthur Grimsdell. George possessed a distinctive running action described as 'bobbing', had a fine eye for the scoring chance, also - despite a moderate stature - had heading ability. A famous exploit that underlined powerful shooting occurred in September 1920 when he broke the net when playing for Wolves. George worked in the printing industry and attained the venerable age of 96 years, 8 months.

GAULT, W(illiam) Ernest

(Everton)

Born: Wallsend, 20 Sep. 1889
Died: 1980
1919: 5-6½, 11-4

Career: Jarrow Caledonians; Everton 1912; Stockport County cs 1913; Everton again Feb. 1917; Cardiff City May 1920; Stockport County again Dec. 1920; New Brighton briefly cs 1922.

Other Honour: (Stockport Co.) FL Div.3 (North) champions 1922
England reserve Vs. Scotland 26 Apr. and 3 May 1919)

Centre/inside-forward. Short but compactly built inside man with skill, speed and marksmanship.

Gault's best years unfortunately coincided with those of the Great War. In seasons 1915/16 to 1918/19 inclusive he aggregated for Stockport and Everton 125 goals in 130 matches, a truly remarkable return. Such form in peacetime would surely have brought high representative honours.

MITCHELL, Archibald P.
(Queens Park Rangers

Born: Smethwick, Staffs. 15 Dec. 1885
Died: Apr. 1949
1919: 5-8½, 12-0
Career: Junior football to Aston Villa 1905; Queen's Park Ragners Aug 1907; Brentford as player/manager Aug. 1921 (last senior appearance 1921/22) - Dec. 1924 staying as a club scout until 1925; worked as a coach on the continent 1926, returning to manage Dartford to 1930; Queen's Park Rangers' coach to reserves 1930 and then their manager Nov. 1931 - Apr. 1933.

Other Honours: Southern League (6 app.)
(QPR) Southern League champions 1912
(England reserve Vs. Wales 11 Oct. 1919)

Centre-half. A right-half at Villa and during his first Rangers' years. He became a regular pivot in 1911, developing into one of the best in the land, strong in all the role's demands. Also Rangers' most influential player, a quality carried into his managerial appointments. Made 467 first team appearances for QPR, scoring 22 goals. Before turning professional, twice played for the Birmingham FA against Scotland and so-called junior internationals.

THOPRE, Levy *
(Burnley)
Born: Seaham Harbour, Co. Durham 18 Nov. 1889
Died: 26 Feb. 1935
1919: 5-7, 10-5
Career: Seaham Harbour FC; Blackpool 1911; Burnley Nov. 1913 (£750); Blackburn Rovers Feb. 1920 (£3,000); Lincoln City Sep. 1922; Rochdale June 1924 - 1926. Subsequently endured a long illness and a benefit was organised for him in 1934 which took place at Blackpool's ground.

(England reserve Vs. Wales 18 Oct 1919)

Wing-half who played mainly on the right early in his first-class career, moving to the other flank in Dec. 1921. Not only a class performer, Thorpe was also remarkably consistent and injury free - several times being a seasonal 'ever-present'. Unlucky though, in the matter of representative and club honours. For example was once selected for the Football League but having to withdraw through illness. A worker and schemer quick to exploit openings.

* Some sources spell his christian name as Levi but a facsimile reproduction of his signature shows the correct version to be Levy.

THE CLUBS WHO SUPPLIED THE PLAYERS

and the

REFEREES

There is little or no record of clubs who didn't operate or grounds that were closed during the period of World War One, but 28 different clubs provided the players who took part in, or were selected as reserves, for the four 1919 England Victory international matches.

THE CLUBS and the PLAYERS

ARSENAL (1) - Williamson
ASTON VILLA (1) - Hardy
BIRMINGHAM CITY (1) - Ball
BLACKBURN ROVERS (3) - Duckworth, Hodkinson, Shea
BOLTON WANDERERS (1) - Smith, Joe
BRADFORD PARK AVENUE (1) - Turnbull
BRENTFORD (1) - E.H. Hendren
BURNLEY (2) - Thorpe *, Watson
CHELSEA (1) - Whittingham
DERBY COUNTY (1) - Bagshaw
EVERTON (3), Fleetwood, Gault *, Grenyer
HUDDERSFIELD TOWN (1) - Cock
LIVERPOOL (1) - Longworth
MANCHESTER CITY (1) - Barnes
MANCHESTER UNITED (1) - Hilditch
MIDDLESBROUGH (1) - Carr *
MILLWALL (1) - Voicey
NEWCASTLE UNITED (1) - Hudspeth
PORTSMOUTH (1) - A.E. Knight
PRESTON NORTH END (1) - McCall
QUEENS PARK RANGERS (1) - Mitchell *
STOKE CITY (1) - Parker
SUNDERLAND (2) - Buchan, Martin
TOTTENHAM (1) - Grimsdell
WATFORD (1) - Edmonds *
WEST BROMWICH ALBION (1) - Smith, Joe
WEST HAM UNITED (1) - Puddefoot
WOLVERHAMPTON WANDERERS (1) - Brooks

Players marked with an asterisk (*) were named 'reserves'.
Their biographical details appear in 'The Nearly Men' chapter.

Unlike the present, when the names and background of the top referees are well known to football fans, the names of the 'men in the middle' were just another name on the team line-ups page of a match programme during the period of the two World Wars.

The names of the four referees used in the Victory internationals of 1919 were Mr A. Warner (Vs Scotland at Everton 26 April 1919), Alexander A. Jackson (Vs Scotland at Hampden Park 3 May 1919), David J. Sambrook, from Swansea (Vs Wales of Cardiff 11 October 1919) and Frank Leigh, from Hanley (Vs Wales at Stoke 18 October 1919). As far as can be determined these gentlemen had no other claims to fame for, as mentioned above, the match officials received little or no publicity or coverage in newspapers, magazines or match programmes of the time.

PROGRAMME PARADE

As the 1919 Victory internationals and the 1939-40 wartime and Victory internationals are regarded as 'unofficial', details of matches are not included in football annuals, handbooks or general football reference books. Consequently, many collectors of England international programmes are not aware of their existence or, if they are, they know little about the details, especially for those matches played away from Wembley in the provinces.

Collectors of club programmes will be aware that those issued during the war years were generally single page team sheets with little, or no, additional reading matter. This was the result of a severe paper shortage and every effort was made to conserve paper with publications, such as books, magazines and programmes, being 'rationed' by the printers who had to maximise their own limited supplies of paper.

Nevertheless, during the first year or so of each War, the clubs and national associations

responsible for producing programmes for the international matches managed to produce quite respectable multi-page issues.

****

1919

Despite appeals to specialist collectors of international programmes and those who collect programmes of matches played on their favourite club's ground - in the case of the Victory internationals, Everton, Stoke, Cardiff and Hampden Park - it has been impossible to track-down even **one** of the programmes from the four England international matches played in 1919.

Programmes must surely have been produced for the games against Scotland (at Goodison Park and Hampden Park) and Wales (at the Victoria Ground, Stoke and Ninian Park Cardiff), therefore if any copies do still exist, the Authors would be pleased to see any examples.

The programme produced by The Football Association of Wales for the 'first' wartime international - Wales Vs England at Ninian Park, Cardiff on Saturday 11 November 1939 - was a 16-pager with illustrations of 'S.F.Rous Esq.,' Secretary of The Football Association, Ted Robbins Esq., Secretary of the F.A. of Wales', and a panoramic view of Ninian Park. There were also portraits of Conrad Veidt and Valerie Hobson - who were starring in 'The Spy in Black' - which was being shown at the Odeon Cinema, Queen Street, Cardiff for six days commencing Monday 13 November 1939!

Total proceeds of this match - which amounted to £1,406 - were donated to the Red Cross and St. John War Organisations Appeal. The programme also contained numerous messages from the Lord Mayor of Cardiff, Colonel The Rt. Hon. Lord Wigram and club officials, emphasising the importance of the work done by the Red Cross Society and Order of St. John.

With food rationing not yet beginning to bite (if you will pardon the pun), Andrews Cafes in St. Mary Street, Cardiff were able to offer a 'Special Three-Course Lunch for 1/3d (approx. 6p) and 'Special Teas at 9d, 1/2d and 1/5d'.

Hancock's Amber Ale was still available at 4½d (2p) a bottle and The Roath Furniture Company of City Road, Cardiff and Commercial Street, Newport were offering, '£1 per month secures £40 worth of Quality Furniture'.

The complete England line-up, who played as printed in the programme, consisted of players selected from London clubs; and there were six Londoners in the Welsh XI, too!

A week later, on 18 November 1939, Wrexham hosted a match between the same two countries, but this time not one single London club player was included in the England team!

This programme - a 12-page issue costing twopence - proved to be the most elusive to track-down.

It was published by the Wrexham F.C. Supporters Club and the only copy known to exist is in a bound volume held in the F.A. of Wales offices in Wrexham.

FOOTBALL ASSOCIATION OF WALES

ENGLAND

Total Receipts to Hospital Supply Depot Wrexham and District British Red Cross and Order of St. John

INTERNATIONAL MATCH

v. WALES
ON
WREXHAM RACECOURSE
Saturday, Nov. 18, 1939

SOUVENIR PROGRAMME - TWOPENCE

ORDER BORDER
... and you
order the Best

The first wartime international played in England, was staged at St. James' Park, Newcastle on 2 December 1939.

A simple 8-page programme, price one penny (old money!), was produced for the game and scheduled to appear in the game for England at right-back was Sam Barkas, and at outside-left, Eric Brook, who were both with Manchester City. The two England stars were involved in a car crash on the way to the game, and were replaced by the Newcastle pair - Joe Richardson at right back and Tommy Pearson (a Scotsman!) at outside left.

W.Phillips and Co., Ltd. of Wrexham advertised the fact that they were still able to offer pre-war stocks of various blends of tea from 2/6d (12½p) to 3/2d (16p) per lb.

The actual receipts of this Wales Vs England game, which amounted to £1,060, were donated to the Hospital Supply Depot Wrexham and District British Red Cross and Order of St. John.

Brook's injuries, sustained in the car crash, were such that he never played professional football again. Barkas recovered, and although never selected for England again, continued his career after the war and won a Division Two Championship medal, with Manchester City, at the age of 37.

INTERNATIONAL MATCH.

ENGLAND
v.
SCOTLAND

•

ST. JAMES'S PARK,
NEWCASTLE-UPON-TYNE.

OFFICIAL PROGRAMME - 1d.
2nd December, 1939.   Kick-off 2-15 p.m.

****

****

Wembley staged its first wartime international on Saturday 13 April 1940, and a splendid 24-page large format programme - similar to the pre-war Wembley Cup Finals and Internationals - was produced.

It had an attractive patriotic red, white and blue cover - printed on quality glossy paper - and

EMPIRE STADIUM

WEMBLEY

FOOTBALL ASSOCIATION
WARTIME
INTERNATIONAL MATCH
ENGLAND v. WALES

SATURDAY APRIL 13 · 1940

OFFICIAL PROGRAMME ● SIXPENCE

contained complete biographical pen pictures of all players in both the England and Wales teams.

The only change to England's programmed line-up was Ken Willingham (Huddersfield Town) who came in for 'Sgt. Instr. J.Mercer (Everton)', at right-half, and this was young 'Gunner Denis Compton's' debut for England.

****

The following month the England party travelled up to Glasgow to meet the 'Auld Enemy' at Hampden Park in the final international match of the 1939-40 season.

The Scots spared no expense in their programme production, producing a superb 16-page illustrated issue - printed on high quality glossy paper throughout - for just 3d, half the cost of Wembley's first wartime issue!

Sam Bartram was programmed to appear in goal for England, but was replaced - at the last minute - by Vic Woodley (Chelsea) when the Charlton custodian could not obtain release from his RAF duties.

****

Official Programme
of the
RED CROSS
International
SCOTLAND
ENGLAND

HAMPDEN PARK
MOUNT FLORIDA · GLASGOW
SATURDAY
11th MAY, 1940
KICK-OFF · · 3 p.m.
PRICE 3D

The first England international of the season was against Scotland and played at St. James' Park, Newcastle, again.

The official programme, price 1d, was a simple 4-page single sheet issue, giving just the team line-ups.

This is, without doubt, the scarcest of the England 'home' wartime international programmes.

****

When Nottingham Forest staged the England Vs Wales match, at their City Ground on Saturday 26 April 1941, they produced a large 8-page illustrated issue with an inner cover announcing 'The Nottingham Forest News and Official Programme' and the familiar Nottingham Co-operative Society Ltd. advertisement of a footballer heading a ball. The programme had an attractive outer cover announcing 'Souvenir Programme' and featuring a portrait of the Wolves centre-half, and England captain, Stan Cullis.

****

The 'War Charities International' between Scotland and England at Hampden Park, saw a 20-page issue, costing 3d, and edited by Alan Breck of 'The Evening Times'.

One of the advertisements in the programme gave details of a succulent meal in war-torn Britain - Quite a feast for 3/9d (19p)!

****

The final match of the 1940-41 season was played between Wales and England at Ninian Park on 7 June 1941. The programme produced, price one penny, was a 4-page single sheet with just the team line-ups, surrounded by various local advertisements.

EMPIRE
STADIUM
WEMBLEY
(Managing Director: A. J. ELVIN)

OCTOBER 4, 1941.
Kick Off 3 p.m.

ASSOCIATION FOOTBALL
MATCH

ENGLAND
 v.
SCOTLAND

IN AID OF WAR CHARITIES

OFFICIAL PROGRAMME SIXPENCE

AIR RAID PRECAUTIONS
In the event of an Air Raid Alert, in the course of which information is given by the Spotters that Enemy Aircraft are in the immediate vicinity of the Stadium, an announcement will be made over the loudspeakers.
Spectators will then be requested to leave the enclosures and make their way quietly to the Circulating Corridors under the Stands, as directed by the Stewards and Officials.
Those wishing to leave the Stadium may do so by any of the usual Exits.

SAT. OCTOBER 25th 1941.   OFFICIAL PROGRAMME PRICE 3d.

BIRMINGHAM
FOOTBALL   **CLUB**

H. MORRIS (*Chairman*)   Directors: L. J. MORRIS
W. A. CAMKIN   D. WISEMAN   H. DARE.
Secretary: S. F. L. RICHARDS.   J. WOOLMAN   St. Andrew's Ground, Birmingham.

This afternoon we welcome to the battle-scarred St. Andrew's Ground the representatives and officials of the English and Welsh Football Associations, their distinguished guests, and the players and officials engaged in the Match. St. Andrew's has not previously been chosen for an International. On a particular morning last November, a gathering such as to-day's would have been hard to imagine, but thanks to many willing helpers and the efforts of Secretary S. F. L. Richards—who has made the arrangements without in any way interfering with his whole time A.F.S. duties—many difficulties have been overcome.

The Prime Minister's presence and that of other members of the War Cabinet, at Wembley three weeks ago, testified to the fact that a limited amount of relaxation is essential to the Nation's War Effort. A rousing game this afternoon will be a tonic for next week's "production" efforts.

We congratulate our players, "Billy" Hughes and Donald Dearson in once more representing their country this afternoon. Frankly, a Welsh team without a "Blues" player would look a little strange. Congratulations also to Fred Harris (England Reserve) and W. Kendrick (Welsh Team Trainer).

AIR RAID PRECAUTIONS.

In the event of an air raid warning during the Match, spectators are requested to carry out instructions which will at once be communicated over the loud speakers. Those wishing to leave the Ground to proceed direct to their homes may do so, but should not use the street shelters in the vicinity of the Ground.

Four months later, on 4 October 1941, Wembley charged 6d (2½p) for their small 4-page single sheet issue for the England match against Scotland.

Although it was printed on glossy paper, there was no reading matter, apart from an 'Air Raid Precautions' notice, the 'Programme of Music', the team line-ups, a full-page Bovril advertisement and an announcement that Belgium would be playing Holland in 'Another great International Match at Wembley - Saturday 11 October 1941'.

****

St. Andrews, Birmingham was the venue for England's match against Wales on 25 October 1941.

This was the first international to be played at Birmingham City's ground and the programme produced was a small 4-page single sheet issue, price 3d.

****

Back at Wembley, on 17 January 1942, England met Scotland again in a match for 'Mrs Churchill's *"Aid to Russia"* Fund'. The programme was similar to that produced for the match played earlier in the season and, again, it was printed on glossy art paper.

****

The shortage of paper was beginning to bite and this was reflected in Scotland's programme for the third meeting of the season against England, at Hampden Park on Saturday 18 April 1942.

Although only a single sheet of paper, measuring just 10" x 8", the canny Scotts managed to turn this into a 6-pager issue, price 3d, by folding the sheet into three and printing it on both sides.

****

For the 'Red Cross and War Charities International', between Wales and England at Ninian Park, Cardiff, on 9 May 1942, the F.A. of Wales produced a 4-page single sheet programme, price one penny.

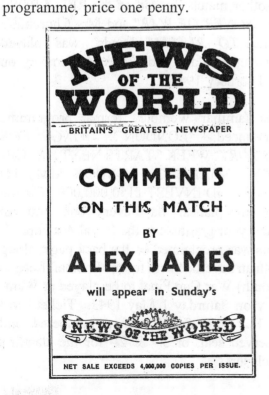

There was no additional reading matter, other than the team line-ups and advertising, but the back page announced *"Comments on this Match by Alex James will appear in Sunday's NEWS OF THE WORLD".*

****

WASTE PAPER SALVAGE

If you do not wish to retain this programme, or the part of your ticket you keep after entering the Stadium, please place them in any one of the many receptacles provided for clean waste paper, as you leave the ground.

You will find these receptacles at various points around the Stadium corridors and at the Exit gates.

Clean waste paper is a sinew of war and your co-operation will be appreciated.

The next England international was played five months later on 10 October 1942, when Scotland were the visitors to Wembley, again.

The usual 4-page single sheet programme was produced with an announcement regarding the recycling of waste paper - This probably accounts for the shortage of certain wartime programmes more than 50 years on!

****

INTERNATIONAL MATCH

ENGLAND

v.

WALES

MOLINEUX GROUNDS, WOLVERHAMPTON

Saturday, October 24th, 1942

KICK-OFF 3-0 P.M.

OFFICIAL PROGRAMME - TWOPENCE

Paulton Bros., Printers, Berry Street, Wolverhampton.

Two weeks later, Wales were England's opponents at Wolverhampton Wanderers' Molineux Grounds.

The programme was a single sheet 4-pager, price two pence, with a view of the Ground on the front cover, portraits of Stan Cullis and Bryn Jones on page 2 and the team line-ups on the back page.

****

Another match 'In Aid of the RED CROSS *"PRISONER OF WAR"* and Mrs Churchill's *"AID TO RUSSIA"* Funds' was played between England and Wales at Wembley on 27 February 1943.

The familiar Wembley format programme announced:- "LONDON'S *"WINGS FOR VICTORY"* WEEK STARTS NEXT SATURDAY - March 6-13. LONDON AIMS TO SAVE AND INVEST £150,000,000. Fill the sky with planes! Save every 'bob' you can show your gratitude to the Royal Air Force!'. This was proclaimed on the back page, along with an advertisement for the Football League (South) War Cup Final to be played at Wembley on Saturday 1 May 1943. Tickets cost £1.1s., 10/6 & 6/-, for a numbered and reserved seat, or 3/- & 2/- for the standing enclosures.

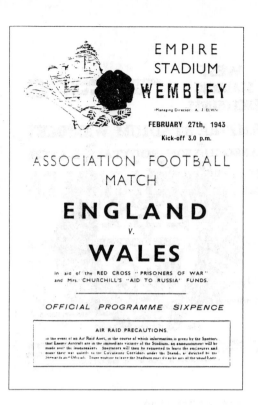

****

More than 100,000 spectators packed into Hampden Park for the match against England on 17 April 1943 and the programme was a 6-page single sheet issue.

Leslie Compton (left-back) and Denis Compton (outside-left) were included in the England line-up - the first brothers to figure in an England team since the days of the Walters brothers - 'A.M.' and 'P.M.'- back in the 1880's.

****

The programme for the 'Red Cross Prisoners of War and Aid to Russia Funds' international between Wales and England at Cardiff on 8 May 1943, was, again, just a single sheet 4-pager with no reading matter - apart from the team line-ups and advertisements.

****

Eighty thousand spectators were at Wembley for the England Vs Wales match, in aid of 'H.R.H. The Duke of Gloucester's Red Cross and St. John Fund', played on 25 September 1943.

The 4-page single sheet programme cost sixpence and England included a virtually 'unknown' goalkeeper - Andy Roxburgh of Blackpool, who was a member of the Fire Service.

Roxburgh conceded three goals, but England's forwards rattled in eight, to give them an 8-3 victory - the highest aggregate score in a wartime international.

WEST STANDING ENCLOSURES

ENTER AT TURNSTILES (See Plan on back) G

EMPIRE STADIUM, WEMBLEY

ASSOCIATION FOOTBALL MATCH

ENGLAND v WALES

SATURDAY, SEPTEMBER 1943

Kick-off 3 p.m.

This portion to be retained until the finish of the match, when it should be deposited in one of the Paper Salvage receptacles as you leave the Ground.

****

Maine Road was the venue for the England match against Scotland on 16 October 1943, and the Manchester club produced for the game a 4-page single sheet programme, costing just one penny.

Half the front page and the two inside pages were devoted to articles on the game, with the team line-ups confined to the back cover of the programme.

The 60,000 all-ticket crowd was thrilled by England's 8-0 win, with Everton's Tommy Lawton scoring four and Raich Carter (Sunderland) even missing a penalty!

****

ONE PENNY

MANCHESTER CITY F.C.L TD.
OFFICIAL PROGRAMME

[Entered at Stationers' Hall.]

ENGLAND
versus
SCOTLAND

ON THE GROUND OF THE
Manchester City F.C.
MAINE ROAD, MOSS SIDE, on

Saturday, October 16, 1943

INTERNATIONAL MATCH

IN the long history of international football rivalry between England and Scotland, dating back to 1872, only once previously has Manchester been honoured by staging the game. That was in season 1925-26, at Old Trafford, when, it will be remembered, Scotland won 1—0, the goal falling to Alec Jackson, then with Huddersfield Town, in the 36th minute.

It is, therefore, with a feeling of great pride to Maine-road habitues that Manchester City ground has been chosen as the venue of to-day's game, and on behalf of the club I take this opportunity of extending a warm welcome to all present to-day. No doubt there will be many amongst the 60,000 to-day who will be seeing Maine-road for the first time.

Maine-road has been the scene of many thrilling and grim football struggles in the past; and although this is war-time when we must be thankful for whatever sport we can get, I do not anticipate to-day's struggle will lack anything of pre-war fervour, or pre-war thrills. In fact, though the uncertainty of players' movements may have the effect of interfering somewhat with the standard of League football in war-time, it has been found that many international matches since the war have produced greater enthusiasm than in many of those contested in pre-war days.

In normal circumstances we should have been anxious to mark to-day's game with a programme of size in keeping with the "big" occasion; but paper restrictions

Printed by Withy Grove Press Limited, Manchester 4

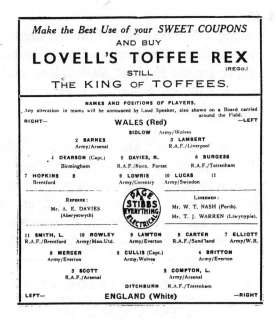
The two countries met again four months later, on 19 February 1944, with the standard Wembley programme being produced. England winning 6-2.

England completed a hat-trick of wins against Scotland, when two goals from Tommy Lawton, and one from Raich Carter, gave them a 3-2 win in front of a partizan crowd of 133,000 Scots at Hampden on 22 April 1944.

The 6-page programme contained the following plea:- *"An RAF officer will be addressing you to-day over the loudspeaker.*

"He will tell you that the RAF want volunteers for flying duties and that men aged 17¼ to 39, no matter their occupations, will be considered for flying". No need for a University education or a string of 'A' levels in those desperate days!

****

England finished their international season, in the usual fashion, at Cardiff beating the Welsh 2-0.

The familiar 4-page single sheet programme costing threepence, was produced by the F.A. of Wales. It is interesting to note that there were blank spaces for the number '8' (inside-right) and number '11' (outside-left) in the Welsh line-up.

Bowles & Son, Wholesale - Retail Tobacconists of 9 James Street, Cardiff were advertising, *"Parcels of Duty-Free Cigarettes and Tobacco can be sent very cheaply and easily to Troops overseas and Prisoners of War - 200 Cigarettes for 4/- (20p) and 4oz. Tobacco for 2/6 (12½p), including packing and postage".*

****

Anfield hosted the first England international of the season, against Wales, on Saturday 16 September 1944.

Liverpool F.C. produced a simple 4-page single sheet programme, costing 2d, which included illustrations of the respective Secretarys of The Football Association and the F.A. of Wales, the Liverpool F.C. Chairman - W.H. McConnell - and the captain's of England (Joe Mercer) and Wales (Billy Hughes).

****

The following month, on 14 October 1944, England were back at Wembley to face Scotland in front of a (home) wartime international record crowd of 90,000. The programme was the usual 4-page single sheet issue.

****

Aston Villa broke away from the single sheet issues when they produced an illustrated 8-pager for the England Vs Scotland match at Villa Park on Saturday 3 February 1945, price sixpence.

As well as the team line-ups and 'Musical Programme' for the afternoon, there were useful detailed biographical pen pictures of all the England and Scotland players taking part in the match. The programme was also completely advert-free - quite a rarity!

****

The familiar 6-page narrow single sheet folded programme was produced for the Scotland Vs England match at Hampden on 14 April 1944.

England won 6-1, thus completing their trio of wins against Scotland for the season, at the same time scoring a total of 15 goals, whilst conceding just 5.

****

Ninian Park, Cardiff hosted the Wales Vs England match on Saturday 5 May 1945, which saw the international debut of Bert Williams (then with Walsall) in the England goal.

Again, the familiar 4-page Welsh programme, but this time with a few paragraphs of 'Programme Notes' on the back page. One of these notes announced:-

WALES v. ENGLAND.

This War Charity International will see the end of War-time Internationals. Should "VE" Day be proclaimed on or before to-day it will also be a Milestone to mark end of European War.

'V.E.' Day was, in fact, proclaimed three days later - 8 May 1945.

****

The Football Association were quick to arrange a celebratory 'Victory' match, between England and France at Wembley on 26 May 1945, and although the programme was still just a single sheet 4-pager, it had a much more attractive cover picturing the Union Jack and French flags super-imposed on a drawing of Wembley stadium.

Although there were no articles or pen pictures of the players taking part in the game, there was a 'Welcome' notice, which read:-

EMPIRE STADIUM **WEMBLEY**
Managing Director · · · A. J. ELVIN

MAY 26th, 1945   Kick-off 3.0 p.m.

INTERNATIONAL
ASSOCIATION FOOTBALL MATCH

ENGLAND
V
FRANCE

In aid of British and French War Charities

OFFICIAL PROGRAMME SIXPENCE

"It is with the greatest pleasure that we welcome to Wembley this afternoon the officials of the Federation Francaise de Football and the members of the French National Team.

"We can imagine nothing more appropriate than that our old friends and allies from France should participate with England in the first "International Association Football match played in this country since the unconditional surrender of our enemy in Europe.

"May this prove to be the first of many meetings between France and England on the football field in the happier years to which we all look forward with a confidence inspired by a true friendship between our two nations".

The first match between England and Ireland, since before the war, was played at Windsor Park on Saturday 14 September 1945. The official programme was a single sheet 4-pager costing twopence.

The following month, on 20 October 1945, West Bromwich Albion hosted the England Vs Wales international and the midlands club produced an 8-pager issue of their large format - 'The Albion News and Official Programme' - for the game, price threepence.

As well as detailed pen pictures of all players in both teams, the programme also included photos of nine players and officials, involved in the match.

****

The Irish made full use of their limited paper supply, by including detailed pen pictures of all the England and Ireland players on the front and back pages of the programme.

****

Belgium were the next foreign visitors to Wembley on Saturday 19 January 1946. This time Wembley issued an 8-page programme with detailed pen pictures of players from both teams and photos from the previous match against France and the England and Belgium F.A. officials.

This match saw the international debut of young Billy Wright (Wolves), who went on to notch-up 105 peacetime appearances for England, in addition to his four Victory internationals in 1946.

EMPIRE STADIUM
WEMBLEY

Managing Director · · · A. J. ELVIN

SATURDAY, JANUARY 19th, 1946

Kick-off 2.30 p.m.

INTERNATIONAL
ASSOCIATION FOOTBALL MATCH

ENGLAND
v.
BELGIUM

Official Programme · - SIXPENCE

* * * * * * * * * * * * * * * * * * * *

The Swiss international team played their first full international in this country when they met England at Stamford Bridge on Saturday 11 May 1946.

* * * * * * * * * * * * * * * * * * * *

The Scots produced a 12-page programme, costing 6d, for the match against England at Hampden on 13 April 1946.

The programme notes pointed out that Scotland had only won two of the fifteen encounters against the 'Auld Enemy' during the war. They must have been particularly pleased to win this Victory international 1-0, with a goal from Manchester United's Jimmy Delaney in front of a record crowd of 139,468!

CHELSEA FOOTBALL & ATHLETIC CO. LTD.

Official Programme

Directors : H. MEARS (Chairman), J. E. C. BUDD C. J. PRATT, H. J. M. BOYER, L. J. MEARS
Manager-Secy. :—Wm. BIRRELL
Ground : STAMFORD BRIDGE, S.W.6. 'Phone : FUL 3421

International
Match

ENGLAND
v.
SWITZERLAND

Saturday, May 11th, 1946

KICK OFF 2.45 P.M.

Official Programme - SIXPENCE

Chelsea issued an 8-page programme, costing sixpence, which contained an interesting feature on 'Football in Switzerland', by John Graydon of Kemsley Newspapers, and pen pictures of both teams - those of the Swiss players being contributed by Willy Meisl.

In addition to the 'official' programme for this game, against Switzerland, a Pictorial Souvenir Programme, price 6d, was also on sale, this announced on the back cover *"This SOUVENIR PROGRAMME is entirely the work of EX-SERVICEMEN".*

It was a single sheet of card, folded in half, with photos of Smith (Aston Villa) and Lawton (Chelsea) on the cover, and a group of nine photos of England players across the centre pages, above the team line-ups. Quite an unusual and scarce item.

The last 'unofficial' international of the 1939-46 period - for which no 'caps' were awarded - was played against France in Paris on Sunday 19 May 1946.

Unfortunately, it has not been possible to find a programme from this game - although it is fairly certain one must have been produced.

It is interesting to note that at right-back for England was Joe Bacuzzi (Fulham), who had the unique distinction of having played in the 'first' and 'last' England internationals of the 1939-46 wartime period.

(If details of the existance of this programme for the match in France, or any of the four 1919 Victory internationals against Scotland and Wales is known, please contact the Authors via the publishers)

ENGLAND'S WARTIME FOOTBALL PHOTO MEMORIES

(Above) England v. Wales - 25 October 1941
(Back): Goslin,Bacuzzi,Marks,Compton D.,Cullis,
(Front): Matthews, Hagan, Hapgood, Welsh,
Mercer,Edelston

(Right) H.M. King George VI being introduced to
Joe Mercer (England v. Wales 27 Feb. 1943).

(Left)   England v. Wales - 7 June 1941.
(Back): Britton, Bacuzzi, Bartram, Cullis,
Male, Buckingham
(Front): Kirchen,Hagen,Hapgood,Goulden,Finch.

(Right) Tommy Lawton scores in the 2-2 draw
with France, at Wembley - 26 May 1945

1939 APPEARANCES and GOALSCORERS 1946

WORLD WAR 2

In the period between the first wartime England international, against Wales at Cardiff on 11 November 1939, up until the final Victory International against France in Paris, on 19 May 1946, a total of 36 England matches were played.

Three England players - Stanley Matthews (29), Joe Mercer (27) and Tommy Lawton (23) - played in more than 20 of these games and Lawton was the leading goalscorer with 24 goals. However, Raich Carter (with 18 goals in 17 appearances) and Don Welsh (12 goals in 9 appearances) also achieved notable 'strike' rates.

Twenty different players - including 'own goals' from Jones (Wales) and Macaulay (Scotland) - contributed to the 98 goals England scored in their 36 matches.

Although 78 players were used by England in these wartime internationals, Joe Bacuzzi (Fulham) was the only player to have the distinction of playing in the 'first' (Vs Wales 11 November 1939) and 'last' (Vs France 19 May 1946) matches of the 6½ year (1939-46) wartime period.

Joe Mercer, who captained his country on 9 occasions, was the only England defender to score a goal in any of these 36 matches. This goal came in the 6-2 win over Scotland at Wembley on 19 February 1944.

Both Tommy Lawton and Don Welsh scored 4 goals in a game and Lawton (twice), Welsh, Carter and Westcott, all scored hat-tricks (see table below). Tommy Lawton had a phenomenal goalscoring run in six consecutive internationals, between 16 October 1943 and 14 October 1944, when he found the net on 12 occasions.

Both Leslie Compton, who played in three different positions - centre forward, right back and left back - in his five appearances and Don Welsh, who turned out at left half, inside left and centre forward, proved their versatility for England.

When the first 'peacetime' international for more than seven years was played against Northern Ireland in Belfast on 28 September 1946, Frank Swift, Laurie Scott, George Hardwick, Billy Wright, Neil Franklin, Tommy Finney and Wilf Mannion - who all made their England debuts during the war years - won their first 'full' caps.

APPEARANCES

Matthews	29		Martin J.R.	2
Mercer	27		Mason	2
Lawton	23		Sproston	2
Cullis	20		Woodley	2
Carter	17		Balmer	1
Hardwick	17		Barrass	1
Hagan	16		Birkett	1
Scott	16		Brook	1
Swift	14		Clifton	1
Bacuzzi	13		Copping	1
Hapgood	13		Crayston	1
Smith L.G.F.	13		Crook	1
Britton	12		Fenton E.	1
Compton D.	12		Fenton M.	1
Franklin	10		L.C. Finch	1
Soo	9		Fisher	1
Welsh	9		Flewin	1
Marks	8		A.H. Gibbons	1
Brown R.A.J.	6		Greenhalgh	1
Goulden	6		Hanson	1
Willingham	6		Harper	1
Compton L.	5		B.Joy	1
M. Edelston	5		Mapson	1
Goslin	4		Mountford	1
Mannion	4		Oakes	1
Westcott	4		Pearson	
Williams	4		Pye	1
Wright	4		Richardson	1
Bartram	3		Rooke	1
Hall W.	3		Rowley J.	1
Kirchen	3		Roxburgh	1
Mortensen	3		Shackleton	1
Mullen	3		Smith G.C.	1
Smith J.R.	3		Stubbins	1
Buckingham	2		Swinburne	1
Ditchburn	2		Taylor F.	1
Elliott	2		Watson	1
Kinsell	2		J.W. Lewis	1

GOALSCORERS

Lawton	24		Matthews	2
Carter	18		Balmer	1
Hagan	13		Birkett	1
Welsh	12		Clifton	1
Westcott	5		M. Edelston	1
Brown R.A.J.	4		Martin J.R.	1
Goulden	3		Mercer	1
Mortensen	3		Pye	1
Smith L.G.F.	3		Jones T.G.(Wales)	1 O.G.
Compton D.	2		Macaulay (Scotland)	1 O.G.

WAR TIME AND VICTORY INTERNATIONALS 1939 – 1946

Season/Date	Opponents	Venue	Attendance	Result	1	2	3	4	5	6	7	8	9	10	11
1939-40															
11 Nov	WALES	Cardiff	28,000	1-1	Woodley	Bacuzzi +	Hapgood (c)	Crayston	Oakes J.	Fenton E.	Smith L.G.F.	Hall G.W.	Compton L.	Goulden (1)	Smith J.R.
18 Nov	WALES	Wrexham	17,000	3-2 *	Swift	Sproston	Crook	Willingham	Cullis (c)	Mercer	Matthews	Martin J.R.(1)	Lawton	Balmer (1)	Brook
2 Dec	SCOTLAND	Newcastle	15,000	2-1	Swinburne	Richardson J.	Greenhalgh	Goslin (c)	B.Harper	Mercer	Matthews	Carter	Lawton (1)	Clifton (1)	Pearson T.W
13 Apr	WALES	Wembley	40,000	0-1	Bartram	Bacuzzi	Hapgood (c)	Willingham	Cullis	Copping	Matthews	Hall G.W.	Westcott	Goulden	Compton D.
11 May	SCOTLAND	Hampden	75,000	1-1	Woodley	Sproston	Hapgood (c)	Willingham	Cullis	Mercer	Matthews	Martin J.R.	Broome	Welsh (1)	Smith J.R.
1940-41															
8 Feb	SCOTLAND	Newcastle	25,000	2-3	Bartram	Bacuzzi	Mountford R.C	Willingham	Cullis (c)	Mercer	Birkett (1)	Mannion	Lawton (1)	Goulden	Hanson A.
26 Apr	WALES	Nottingham	13,016	4-1	Mapson	Bacuzzi	Hardwick	Britton	Cullis (c)	Buckingham	Fisher F.W.	M.Edelston	Welsh (4)	Hagan	Smith J.R.
3 May	SCOTLAND	Hampden	78,000	3-1	Swift	Bacuzzi	Hapgood (c)	Goslin	Cullis	Mercer	Matthews	Mannion	Welsh (2)	Goulden (1)	Compton D.
7 June	WALES	Cardiff	20,000	3-2	Bartram	Bacuzzi	Hapgood (c)	Britton	Cullis	Buckingham	Kirchen	Hagan (2)	Welsh (1)	Goulden	L.C.Finch
1941-42															
4 Oct	SCOTLAND	Wembley	65,000	2-0	Marks	Bacuzzi	Hapgood (c)	Goslin	Cullis	Mercer	Matthews	Mannion	Welsh (1)	Hagan (1)	Compton D.
25 Oct	WALES	Birmingham	25,000	2-1	Marks	Bacuzzi	Hapgood (c)	Goslin	Cullis	Mercer	Matthews	M.Edelston(1)	Welsh	Hagan (1)	Compton D.
17 Jan	SCOTLAND	Wembley	64,000	3-0	Marks	Bacuzzi	Hapgood (c)	Willingham	Cullis	Welsh	Matthews	Mannion	Lawton (2)	Hagan (1)	Compton D.
18 Apr	SCOTLAND	Hampden	75,000	4-5	Marks	Bacuzzi	Hapgood (c)	Willingham	Mason G.W.	Mercer	Matthews	M.Edelston	Lawton (3)	Hagan (1)	Kirchen
9 May	WALES	Cardiff	30,000	0-1	Marks	Scott	Hapgood (c)	Britton	Mason G.W.	Soo	Kirchen	G.W.Hall	Lawton	M.Edelston	Smith L.G.F.
1942-43															
10 Oct	SCOTLAND	Wembley	75,000	0-0	Marks	Bacuzzi	Hapgood (c)	Britton	Cullis	Mercer	Matthews	M.Edelston	Lawton	Hagan	Compton D.
24 Oct	WALES	W'hampton	25,000	1-2	Marks	Hardwick	Hapgood (c)	Britton	Cullis	Mercer	Matthews	Rooke	Lawton (1)	A.H.Gibbons	Mullen
27 Feb	WALES	Wembley	75,000	5-3	Marks	Bacuzzi	Hapgood (c)	Britton	Cullis	Mercer	Matthews	Carter (2)	Westcott (3)	Hagan	Compton D.
17 Apr	SCOTLAND	Hampden	105,000	4-0	Swift	Hardwick	Compton L.	Britton	Cullis (c)	Mercer	Matthews	Carter (2)	Westcott (1)	Hagan	Compton D.(1)
8 May	WALES	Cardiff	25,000	1-1	Swift	Hardwick	Compton L.	Britton	Cullis (c)	Mercer	Matthews	Carter	Westcott (1)	Hagan	Compton D.

* Includes own goal from T.G.Jones.   + Bacuzzi injured, J.W.Lewis substitute.   (c) denotes Captain.   (Where first name initials are given before a surname, this indicates an Amateur player)

Season/Date	Opponents	Result	Attendance	Venue	1	2	3	4	5	6	7	8	9	10	11
1943-44															
25 Sep	WALES	8-3	80,000	Wembley	Roxburgh	Scott	Hardwick	Britton	Cullis (c)	Soo	Matthews	Carter (2)	Welsh (3)	Hagan (2)	Compton D.
16 Oct	SCOTLAND	8-0	60,000	Manchester	Swift	Scott	Hardwick	Britton	Cullis (c)	Mercer	Matthews (1)	Carter (1)	Lawton (4)	Hagan (2)	Compton D.
19 Feb	SCOTLAND	6-2 *	80,000	Wembley	Ditchburn	Scott	Hardwick	Britton	Cullis (c)	Mercer (1)	Matthews	Carter (1)	Lawton (1)	Hagan (2)	Smith L.G.F.
22 Apr	SCOTLAND	3-2	133,000	Hampden	Swift	Compton L.	Taylor F.	Soo	Cullis (c)	Mercer	Matthews	Carter (1)	Lawton (2)	Hagan	Smith L.G.F.
6 May	WALES	2-0	50,000	Cardiff	Ditchburn	Compton L.	Scott	Britton	Cullis (c)	Mercer	Elliott W.	Carter	Lawton (1)	J.F.Rowley	SmithL.G.F.(1)
1944-45															
16 Sep	WALES	2-2	38,483	Anfield	Swift	Scott	Hardwick	Mercer (c)	Flewin	Welsh	Matthews	Carter (1)	Lawton (1)	Mortensen	Mullen
14 Oct	SCOTLAND	6-2	90,000	Wembley	Swift	Scott	Hardwick	Soo	B.Joy	Mercer (c)	Matthews	Carter (1)	Lawton (3)	Goulden (1)	SmithL.G.F.(1)
3 Feb	SCOTLAND	3-2	64,000	Villa Park	Swift	Scott	Hardwick	Soo	Franklin	Mercer (c)	Matthews	Brown R.A.J.(1)	Lawton	Mortensen(2)	Smith L.G.F.
14 Apr	SCOTLAND	6-1	133,000	Hampden	Swift	Scott	Hardwick	Soo	Franklin	Mercer (c)	Matthews(1)	Carter (1)	Lawton (2)	Brown R.A.J.(1)	Smith L.G.F.(1)
5 May	WALES	3-2	25,000	Cardiff	Williams	Scott	Hardwick	Smith G.C.	Franklin	Mercer (c)	Matthews	Carter (3)	Lawton	Brown R.A.J.	Smith L.G.F.
26 May	FRANCE	2-2	60,000	Wembley	Williams	Scott	Hardwick	Soo	Franklin	Mercer	Matthews	Carter (1)	Lawton (1) (c)	Brown R.A.J.	Smith L.G.F.
1945-46															
14 Sep	IRELAND	1-0	45,061	Belfast	Swift	Scott	Kinsell	Soo	Franklin	Mercer (c)	Matthews	Carter	Lawton	Mortensen (1)	Smith L.G.F.
20 Oct	WALES	0-1	56,000	West Brom.	Williams	Scott	Kinsell	Soo	Franklin	Mercer (c)	Matthews	M.Fenton	Stubbins	Barrass	Watson W.
19 Jan	BELGIUM	2-0	85,000	Wembley	Swift	Scott	Hardwick	Wright W.	Franklin	Mercer (c)	Matthews	Pye (1)	Lawton	Brown R.A.J.(1)	Mullen
13 Apr	SCOTLAND	0-1	139,468	Hampden	Swift	Scott	Hardwick	Wright W.	Franklin	Mercer (c)	W.Elliott	Shackleton	Lawton	Hagan	Compton D.
11 May	SWITZERLAND	4-1	75,000	Chelsea	Swift	Scott	Hardwick	Wright W.	Franklin	Johnson W.H.	Matthews	Carter (2)	Lawton (1) (c)	Brown R.A.J.(1)	Smith L.G.F.
19 May	FRANCE	1-2	58,481	Paris	Williams	Bacuzzi	Hardwick	Wright W.	Franklin	Johnson W.H.	Matthews	Carter	Lawton (c)	Hagan (1)	Smith L.G.F.

* Includes own goal by A.Macaulay.   (c) denotes Captain.   (Where first name initials are given before a surname, this indicates an Amateur player)

1939-46 England Wartime & Victory Internationals Summary:

	Pl.	Home					Away				
		W.	D.	L.	F.	A.	W.	D.	L.	F.	A.
Vs. Scotland	16	7	1	1	32	10	4	1	2	21	11
Vs. Wales	15	4	1	3	22	14	4	2	1	13	9
Vs. Northern Ireland	1						1	0	0	1	0
Vs. Belgium	1	1	0	0	2	0					
Vs. France	2	0	1	0	2	2	0	0	1	1	2
Vs. Switzerland	1	1	0	0	4	1					

	Pl.	W.	D.	L.	F.	A.
Summary:	36	22	6	8	98	49

BACUZZI, Guisseppe Luigi Davide ("Joe")

(Fulham and The Army)

(13 England wartime apps.)

Born: Kings Cross, London. 25 Sep. 1916

Died: 1 Feb 1995

1938: 5-9, 11-12

Career: Islington Schools (during which he appeared in the representative schools XI's of both Middx. and London); Tufnell Park (2 seasons plus a few games in Arsenal 'A' team); Fulham (amat.) June 1935, (prof.) April 1936, retired 1956. Assistant trainer until 1965. Later employed by Sainsbury's as a cook.

Other Honour: (Fulham) FL Div.2 Champions 1949.

Right-back, after WW2 moving to the other flank. One of Fulham's longest serving employees, being associated with the Club for an unbroken 30 years. Joe's strengths were a cogent tackle, accurate long passing, and a positional sense that included profitable attacking gambits. Father of David Bacuzzi, a well-known full-back with Arsenal, Manchester City and Reading during the 1960's.

BALMER, John

(Liverpool and The Army)

(1 England wartime app., 1 goal)

Born: Liverpool 6 Feb. 1916

Died: 25 Dec. 1984

1938: 5-9¾, 10-4

Career: Collegiate School, Liverpool; Collegiate Old Boys (represented both Liverpool FA and County FA and also on Everton's books an an amateur); Liverpool FC amateur May 1935, turning prof. the following August; retired cs 1952. In later life owned and ran a contractor's business.

Other Honour: (Liverpool) FL champions 1947

Inside-forward sometimes centre-forward. Usually at inside-right but played inside-left in his wartime international. Came to Liverpool's notice through prolific scoring in the Collegiate Old Boys' cause. Did not lose his scoring touch in the first-class game, in peacetime netting 111 in 313 League and cup-tie matches. This included a 'purple patch' during Nov. 1946 when Jack scored 10 in 3 consecutive FL fixtures. Nephew of William and Robert Balmer, bothers who formed a famous Everton full-back partnership in Edwardian days.

BARRASS, Malcolm Williamson

(Bolton Wanderers)

(1 England wartime app.)

Born: Blackpool, 13 Dec. 1924

1949: 5-10¾, 12-7

Career: Ford Motors (Manchester); Bolton Wanderers early 1944; Sheffield United Sep. 1956 (£5,000); Wigan Athletic as player/manager July 1958 - Jan. 1959; Nuneaton Borough 1959/60 season; Pwllheli early 1961; Hyde United trainer cs 1962.

Other Honours: England (3 'full' apps.)
Football League (2 apps.)
(Bolton Wanderers) FA Cup finalist 1953

Inside-left in his wartime international, subsequently an effective half-back, first as pivot then at left-half. Quickly came to the fore after joining Bolton, a fact demonstrated by his 1946 England selection. As a centre-half, Malcolm was a commanding figure with his fine physique, mobility and skill in the air. Son of Matt Barrass who won honours with the Wednesday and Manchester City during the 'twenties.

BARTRAM, Samuel
(Charlton Athletic and the Royal Air Force)
(3 England wartime apps.)
Born: Simonside, Co. Durham, 22 Jan. 1914
Died: 17 July 1981
1938: 6-0½, 12-5½
Career: Sunderland Schools and then assisted several North-East non-League sides, notably having five spells with Boldon Villa (Reading trial during the third spell), from which club he joined Charlton Atheltic, Sep. 1934; retired Mar. 1956. York City manager Mar. 1956; Luton Town manager July 1960 - June 1962. Subsequently for many years a 'Sunday People' journalist.

Other Honours: (Charlton) FL Div.3 (South) champions 1935
FA Cup winner 1947; finalist 1946

A major figure in Charlton Athletic's rise to the top light in the 1930's and among the finest 'keepers never

to be awarded a full cap. Unorthodox in method - not being averse to an upfield sortie! - Sam was nonetheless wonderfully consistent, finishing with a club record 623 peacetime League and FA Cup appearances. Worked as a miner on leaving school and had a sports shop near to The Valley while still a player.

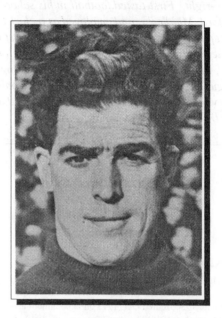

BIRKETT, Ralph James Evans
(Newcastle United and The Army)
(1 England wartime app., 1 goal)
Born: Newton Abbot, Devon, 9 Jan. 1913
1938: 5-9, 11-4

Career: Dartmouth United; Torquay United amateur 1929, turning prof. Mar. 1930; Arsenal Apr. 1933; Middlesbrough Mar. 1935 (£2,000); Newcastle United July 1938 (£5,900); retired 1941.

Other Honours: England (1 'full' cap)
Football League (2 apps.)

Outside-right. First tasted football in his school days at Ashford, Middlesex, and employed as a clerk before taking up the game professionally. Unable to establish a first team place at Highbury, where competition was intense, but did well in the North-east, finishing with a League record of 231 appearances, 63 goals. A speedy wingman possessing guile, and he was dangerous in the vicinity of the opposing goalmouth.

BRITTON, Clifford Samuel
(Everton and The Army)
(12 England wartime apps.)
Born: Hanham, Briston, 29 Aug. 1909
Died: 1 Dec. 1975
1938: 5-10½, 11-2
Career: Hanham Athletic; Hanham United Methodists; Bristol St. George's; Bristol Rovers amateur 1926, turning prof. cs 1928; Everton June 1930; retired Oct. 1945 on appointment as Burnley's manager (until Sep. 1948). Everton manager Sep. 1948 - Feb. 1956; Preston North End manager Aug. 1956 - Apr. 1961; Hull City manager July 1961, becoming that club's General Manager Nov. 1969 until his retirement in Oct. 1971.

Other Honours: England (9 'full' apps.)
Football League (4 apps.)
(Everton) FA Cup winner 1933

Right-half. A most cultured player endowed with all the traditional wing-half skills, especially with his distribution, a facet that could hardly be bettered. Noted, too, as one of the best managerial talents of his day. Unusually in such an uncertain profession, Britton was given a 10-year contract at his last club, Hull City.

BROOK, Eric Fred
(Manchester City)
(1 England wartime app.)
Born: Mexborough, Yorks, 27 Nov. 1907
Died: 29 Mar. 1965
1938: 5-7½, 11-12½
Career: Mexborough Schools; Oxford Road YMCA; Swinton Prims; Mexborough FC; Dearne Valley Old Boys; Wath Athletic; Barnsley Feb. 1926 (£200); Manchester City Mar. 1928 (£4000, which fee included Fred Tilson, another future England cap); retired during WW2.

Other Honours: England (18 'full' apps.)
Football League (7 apps.)
(Manchester City) FL champions 1937
FA Cup winner 1934; finalist 1933

Outside-left. Famed for explosive shooting and aptitude for popping up anywhere where the action was. Remarkably consistent and injury free too : at the time of an appendicitis operation (Nov. 1937) it was the first time he had been absent for anything other than international calls. Latterly a crane driver in Manchester.

BROOME, Frank Henry
(Aston Villa)
(1 England wartime app.)

Born: Berkhampstead, Herts, 11 June 1915
Died: 5 Sep. 1994
1938: 5-7¾, 10-1

Career: Herts. Schools football; Boxmoor United; Berkhampstead Town; Aston Villa Nov. 1934; Derby County Sep. 1946; Notts County Oct. 1949; Brentford July 1953; Crewe Alexandra Oct. 1953; Shelbourne Feb. 1955; Notts County assistant trainer cs 1955, acting manager Jan. - May 1957 and assistant manager to Dec. 1957; Exeter City manager/coach Jan. 1958; Southend United manager May - Dec. 1960; Bankstown (NSW) manager/coach July 1961 - Oct. 1962; Corinthians (Sydney) manager/coach later in 1962; Melita Eagles (Sydney) part-time coach early in 1967; Exeter City manager Apr. 1967 - Feb. 1969, subsequently coaching for a short time in the Middle East.

Other Honours: England (7 'full' apps.)
(Aston Villa) FL Div.2 champions 1938
(Notts County) FL Div.3 (South) champions 1950

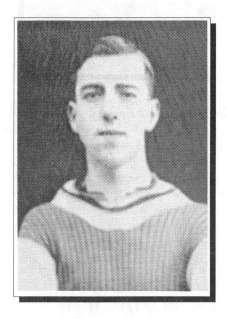

Centre-forward in his wartime international and had often appeared in that position for Villa. In fact extremely versatile, being able to occupy any of the five attack berths. Turned down by both 'Spurs and Arsenal as 'too small', Broome more than compensated for a slight build by his dash, bravery and goal scoring potential. Of special note, he played in the first class game until nearly 40.

BROWN, R(obert) Albert J(ohn) ("Sailor")
(Charlton Athletic and the Royal Air Force)
(6 England wartime apps., 4 goals)

Born: Great Yarmouth, 7 Nov. 1915
1938: 5-8, 10-5

Career: Gorleston FC; Charlton Atheltic Aug. 1934; Nottingham Forest May 1946 (£6,750); Aston Villa Oct. 1947 (£10,000); retired through injury June 1949; Gorleston player/manager Aug. 1949 - cs 1956. Later scouted for Aston Villa

Other Honours: FA tourist to South Africa 1939 (played in one Test) (Charlton Athletic) FA Cup finalist 1946

Inside-forward who, like so many, was robbed of his best footballing years by the War. Nicknamed Sailor, not for any particular association with the sea but because of a distinctive rolling gait. Attracted two notable fees (by immediate post-war period standards). Brown was enormously talented - a probing, cogent attacker ever alive to the scoring chance. His post-war aggregate League record reads 76 appearances, 26 goals. After leaving football had several jobs including running a sports shop, a turf accountant, a holiday camp sports organiser and, lastly, as a timber merchant.

BUCKINGHAM, Victor Frederick
(Tottenham Hotspur and the Royal Air Force)
(2 England wartime apps.)

Born: Greenwich, 23 Oct. 1915
Died: 26 Jan. 1995
1938: 5-10, 11-2

Career: Greenwich Schools; Tottenham Hotspur amateur 1931, turning prof. June 1934 (Northfleet - Spurs 'nursery' club for development - season 1934/35); retired June 1951 on appointment as Bradford's manager; West Bromwich Albion manager Feb. 1953; Ajax (Amsterdam) manager May 1959; Sheffield Wednesday manager June 1961 - Apr. 1964; Ajax manager/coach for second spell July 1964; Fulham manager Jan. 1965 - Jan. 1968; Ethnikos (Athens) manager/coach May 1968; Barcelona manager Dec. 1969 - July 1971; Seville manager 1972, then completed his career with a second spell in Greece managing Ethnikos before retiring to Bognor Regis.

Left-half with subsequent considerable experience at left-back. An attractive, blond haired performer of athletic build, stylish and effective in both positions. Successful and long-lasting in management too. A premonition of this can be discerned in Buckingham's earliest off-the-field appointments as chief coach to the Middlesex FA and the coaching of Pegasus FC to their 1951 Amateur Cup triumph.

CARTER, Horatio Stratton ("Raich")
(Sunderland and the Royal Air Force)
(17 England wartime apps. 18 goals)
Born: Hendon, Sunderland, 21 Dec. 1913
Died: 9 Oct. 1994
1938: 5-8, 10-6
Career: Sunderland Schools; Whitburn St. Mary's; Esh Winning; Sunderland Forge; Sunderland FC amateur Nov. 1930, turning prof. Nov. 1931; Derby County Dec. 1945 (£8,000) after guesting for that club during WW2; Hull City as player/assistant manager Mar. 1948 (£6,000), becoming player/manager May 1948, resigning the managership Sep. 1951 and continuing to play until Apr. 1952; Cork Athletic Jan. 1953; Leeds United manager May 1953 - June. 1958; Mansfield Town manager Feb. 1960; Middlesbrough manager Jan. 1963 - Feb. 1966.

Other Honours: England (13 'full' apps.)
England schoolboy international (4 apps.)
Football League (4 apps.)
(Sunderland)   FL champions 1936
                      FA Cup winner 1937
(Derby County) FA Cup winner 1946
(Hull City) FL Div.3 (North) champions 1949
(Cork Athletic) FA of Ireland Cup winner 1953

Inside-right in all his England wartime games but equally well acquainted - and effective - at inside-left. Universally recognised as among the all-time great players. A past master of ball control, superb tactically and a powerful, accurate shot. Steering Hull City to their 1949 Northern Section championship was a managerial triumph. No mean cricketer either, assisting Durham in the Minor Counties and thrice appearing for Derbyshire in 1946.

CLIFTON, Henry
(Newcastle United)
(1 England wartime app., 1 goal)
Born: Marley Hill, Newcastle -u- Tyne, 28 May 1914
1938: 5-8, 11-7
Career: Lintz Colliery (West Bromwich Albion amateur Sep. 1932); Scotswood; Chesterfield Aug. 1933; Newcastle United June 1938 (£8,000); Grimsby Town Jan. 1946 (£2,500); Goole Town cs 1949.

Other Honour: (Chesterfield) FL Div.3 (North) champions 1936

Inside-left for his 1939 England appearance, often on the other flank and sometimes centre-forward during his first-class career.

A strong performer, difficult to dispossess. Much fancied while with Chesterfield, returning to Geordieland after five years for a large fee by 1938 standards. Returned to that area permanently following post-war engagements either side of the Humber.

Career: Hampstead Town, Arsenal amateur Sep. 1932, assisting Nunhead while on the club's ground staff, before signing as a prof. in May 1935; retired late 1950.

Other Honours: (Arsenal) FL champions 1948
FA Cup winner 1950

Outside-left, unusually well built for the berth, thus posing a bigger threat than his able orthodoxy automatically posed. Even more famous, of course, as the Middlesex and England cricketer whose deeds after the War made history. These included 78 test appearances and, in 1947, hitting 18 centuries and finishing with an astonishing average of 90.85 runs per innings. Brother of L.H. Compton (below). Denis' good looks also became very famous at the time advertising Brylcream brilliantine. After retirement, worked as a cricket and football journalist and as director of an advertising agency. Awarded the CBE in 1958.

COMPTON, Denis Charles Scott
(Arsenal and The Army)
(12 England wartime apps., 2 goals)
Born: Hendon, Middlesex, 23 May 1918
1948: 5-10, 11-10

COMPTON, Leslie Harry
(Arsenal, The Army and Wartime Police force)
(5 England wartime apps.)
Born: Woodford, Essex, 12 Sep. 1912
Died: 27 Dec. 1984
1948: 6-1½, 13-2

Career: Hendon schoolboy football; Bell Lane Old Boys (Hendon); Hampstead Town circa 1929; Arsenal amateur Aug. 1930, turning prof. Feb. 1932; retired July 1953, then serving on Arsenal's coaching staff until Feb. 1956.

Other Honours: England (2 'full' app.)
Football League (1 app.)

(Arsenal) FL champions 1948
FA Cup winner 1950

Right/left-back pre-war then centre-forward for his initial (1940) England appearance, his later one being at full-back. Played at centre-half post-war. A strong unyielding player, hard tackling and using his height to dominant effect in headwork. Elder brother of Denis above, Les himself assisting Middlesex CCC 1938-56 (272 matches) as a batsman/wicket-keeper/pace bowler. Reckoned on his first 'full' cap to be England's oldest debutant, but this distinction may belong to Alex. Morten, who was honoured in 1873. After leaving football, Les worked as a wine company's representative. The Compton brothers had a sister who was a noted athlete.

COPPING, Wilfred

(Leeds United and The Army)
(1 England wartime app.)

Born: Middlecliffe, Barnsley, 17 Aug. 1907
Died: June 1980
1938: 5-7, 10-13

Career: Dearne Valley Old Boys; Middlecliffe & Darfield Rovers; Leeds United amateur Mar. 1929, turning prof. 1930; Arsenal June 1934 (£6,000); Leeds United Mar. 1939; retired during WW2. Coached in Belgium 1945-46; Southend United trainer cs 1946; Bristol City trainer July 1954; Coventry City trainer Nov. 1956 - May 1959.

Other Honours: England (20 'full' apps.)
Football League (2 apps.)
(Arsenal) FL champions 1935, 1938
FA Cup winner 1936

Left-half. A former miner who became the archetypal 'hard man' famed for a blockbuster tackle and an equally formidable shoulder charge. At the same time Wilf's canny passing was admirable and he could exploit a throw-in of great length. Once in the paid ranks, he clocked up a total of 337 League appearances in 9 seasons, averaging 37 - all but one season in the top flight - a tribute to his fitness and freedom from injury.

CRAYSTON, W(illiam) John

(Arsenal and the Royal Air Force)
(1 England wartime app.)

Born: Grange-over-Sands, Lancs., 9 Oct. 1910
Died: 31 Dec. 1992
1938: 6-0¼, 13-4

Career: Barrow-in-Furness schools football; Ulverston Town; Barrow Aug. 1928; Bradford May 1930; Arsenal May 1934 (£5,250 at the time a Park Avenue record); retired through injury 1943 and appointed Arsenal's assistant manager; Arsenal manager Dec. 1956 - May 1958; Doncaster Rovers manager June 1958, becoming their secretary/manager Mar. 1959 - June 1961.

Other Honours: England (8 'full' apps.)
Football League (1 app.)
(Arsenal) FL champions 1935, 1938
FA Cup winner 1936

Right-half with experience at centre-half during his Barrow and Bradford days. In style contrasted with his dour Arsenal wing-half partner (Wilf Copping above). Jack had lithe grace and height that usually gave command in headwork. Employed as a Streetly (Birmingham) shopkeeper from 1961, retiring in 1974.

CROOK, Walter
(Blackpool Rovers and The Army)
(1 England wartime app.)

Born: Whittle-le-Woods, Lancs., 28 Apr. 1913
Died: 27 Dec. 1988
1938: 5-10½, 11-0

Career: Blackburn Nomads; Blackburn Rovers Jan. 1931; Bolton Wanderers May 1947; retired through injury cs 1948. Ajax (Amsterdam) manager/coach 1948/49; Accrington Stanley trainer/coach Mar. 1951 before being upgraded to manager/coach June 1951 and secretary/manager July 1952 - Feb. 1953; coached in Holland again briefly before appointment as Wigan Athletic's manager Oct. 1954 - cs 1955; subsequently serving as Preston North End's coach for many years until retiring in Apr. 1969.

Other Honour: (Blackburn Rovers) FL Div.2 champions 1939

Left-back. Gave outstanding service to Blackburn Rovers. After gaining a first team place in 1934/35 he had a great run of over 190 consecutive League appearances right up to the outbreak of war, a tribute to both his fitness and consistency. In style Crook was of assertive bent, revelling in physical contact. He skippered Blackburn to their 1939 championship. A successful initiation to the management side of the game in Holland could not be repeated at Accrington because of their limited resources.

CULLIS, Stanley
(Wolverhampton Wanderers and The Army)
(20 England wartime apps.)

Born: Ellesmere Port, Cheshire, 25 Oct. 1915
1939: 5-10, 11-8

Career: Ellesmere Port Schools; Ellesmere Port Wednesday; Wolverhampton Wanderers Feb. 1934 - Aug. 1947 when appointed the club's assistant manager and then their secretary/manager June 1948 - Sep. 1964; Birmingham City manager Dec. 1965 - Mar. 1970.

Other Honours: England (12 'full' apps.)
Football League (3 apps.)
(Wolves) FA Cup finalist 1939

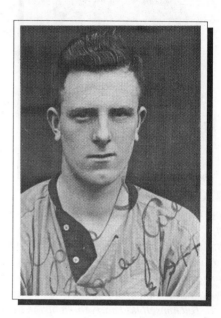

Centre-half of all round prowess, among the greatest England has produced. Magnificent in heading, ground work and distribution and quite unyielding. Outstanding as Wolves' manager too; in his 16-year reign the club picked up three League championships and won the FA Cup twice. On leaving the game became managing/director of a photographic agency and latterly worked as a football columnist.

DITCHBURN, Edwin George
(Tottenham Hotspur and the Royal Air Force)
(2 England wartime apps.)

Born: Gillingham, Kent, 24 Oct. 1921
1949: 6-0¾, 12-9

Career: Northfleet schools football; Northfleet Paper Mills; Tottenham Hotspur amateur cs 1937, sent to the club's nursery (Northfleet FC) 1938, and turned prof. May 1939; Romford Apr. 1959 (player/manager July 1959 - Mar. 1962); Brentwood Aug. 1965. Later a Romford sports outfitter.

Other Honours: England (6 'full' apps.)
England 'B' (2 apps.)
Football League (6 apps.)
(Spurs) FL champions 1951
FL Div.2 champions 1950

Goalkeeper unfortunate in being a contemporary of Swift and Bert Williams, otherwise his cap's tally would surely have been greater. Quite brilliant and consistent with it (had a run of 247 consecutive League appearances at one juncture), his sizeable frame no bar to acrobatics. Son of a Kent heavy-weight boxing champion, Ted himself had early thoughts on taking up the sport seriously. Doubtless his large hands would have been as handy as they were in soccer.

EDELSTON, Maurice
(Reading and The Army)
(5 England wartime apps., 1 goal)
Born: Hull, 27 Apr. 1918
Died: 30 Jan. 1976
1949: 5-8, 10-4
Career: Hull schoolboy football; Wimbledon in the 1930's, assisting London University 1936-39 and signing amateur forms for Fulham May 1935; Brentford Dec. 1937 and Reading May 1939. Turned prof. for Reading July 1947; Northampton Town July 1952 (approx. £2,000); retired cs 1954.

Other Honours: Gt. Britain (1 app. 1936 Olympic games vs. China)
England amateur international (9 apps.)

Inside-forward. One of the 'thirties crack amateurs'. Turned 29 when he took the professional ticket but he *had sampled League fare at Fulham and Brentford, in the top flight with the latter. From soccer stock - son of Joe Edelston, well known as a player and manager - Maurice packed a shot both accurate and very hard. In later years famous and popular as a BBC commentator, his early demise much deplored.*

ELLIOTT, William Bethwaite
(West Bromwich Albion and The Army)
(2 England wartime apps.)

Born: Harrington, Cumberland, 6 Aug. 1919
Died: 24 Nov. 1966
1939: 5-7½,
Career: Junior football to Carlisle United on amateur forms Nov. 1936; Wolverhampton Wanderers July 1937 (Dudley Town on loan 1937/38 season); Bournemouth & Boscombe Athletic May 1938; West Bromwich Albion Dec. 1938; Bilston United as player/manager Aug. 1951; retired 1954.

Outside-right among West Bromwich Albion's all time stars. Highly mobile yet finely retaining command of the ball with considerable shooting power in his right foot. Scored 40 goals in 182 peacetime League and FA Cup matches for Albion, an excellent return for a wingman. He was a Birmingham licensee at the time of his death.

FENTON, Edward Benjamin A.
(West Ham United and The Army)
(1 England wartime app.)
Born: Forest Gate, London, 9 Nov. 1914
Died: 14 July 1992
1938: 5-10½, 11-6
Career: West Ham Schools; Colchester Town; West Ham United amateur 1930, turning prof. 1932; Colchester United player/manager May 1946; West Ham United manager Aug. 1950 - Mar. 1961; Southend United manager Mar. 1961 - May 1965.

Other Honours: England schoolboy international (1 app.)
FA tourist to South Africa 1939, thrice appearing against the South African national XI.
He also played for England in an unofficial match against Switzerland in 1945.

A true Hammers loyalist with 16 years on the playing staff plus 11 in the managerial chair. Ted had played centre-forward for both Essex and London Schools but as a senior converted to being a wing-half/inside-forward. A sound, thoughtful performer as well as a versatile one. Was in charge at (then) non-League Colchester when the side made its celebrated 1948 FA Cup run, and at West Ham when they regained long-lost Division One status. On leaving football he worked as a licensee and ran a Brentwood sports shop before retiring to Gloucestershire. Elder brother of the late Benny Fenton, whose career with West Ham and other League clubs covered two decades.

FENTON, Michael
(Middlesbrough and the Royal Air Force)
(1 England wartime app.)
Born: Stockton-on-Tees, 30 Oct. 1913
1938: 5-9, 11-0
Career: Stockton-on-Tees Schools; South Bank East End; Middlesbrough Mar. 1933, player/coach Jan. 1949 retiring as a player cs 1951 and then remaining on the club's coaching staff until cs 1966.

Other Honours: England (1 'full' app.)
FA tourist to South Africa 1939, thrice appearing against the South African national XI.
He also played for England in an unofficial match against Switzerland in 1945.

Centre-forward able to take an inside berth also - he was at inside-right in the England wartime match. Michael followed in a long succession of distinguished

Middlesbrough centre-forwards that included such luminaries as Alf Common, George Elliott, Andy Wilson and George Camsell. He possessed physical strength, two-footed ability and outstanding speed, even from a standing start. Outside football he ran a Stockton-on-Tees newsagency.

FINCH, Lester Charles

(Barnet and the Royal Air Force)
(1 England wartime app.)

Born: Hadley, Herts., 26 Aug. 1909
Career: Schoolboy football; Hadley FC 1925; Barnet 1928-1948. During WW2 assisted Chelsea, Wolverhampton Wanderers, West Bromwich Albion, Nottingham Forest, Walsall and Bournemouth & Boscombe Athletic. He signed amateur forms for Arsenal in Apr. 1933 but made no senior appearances for that club.

Other Honours: G.Britain, playing twice in the 1936 Olympic Games
England amateur international (16 apps.)
(Barnet) FA Amateur Cup winner 1946
FA Amateur Cup finalist 1948
FA tourist to South Africa 1939, twice playing against the South Africa national XI

Outside-left. One of the great amateurs of his day : small physically but cogently adept in all aspects of forward play, and, of course, extremely durable as the above career length indicates. Besides the '39 South Africa tour, he toured Europe at different times with Athenian League and London FA parties and in 1937, New Zealand and Australia with the England amateur party. Lester's working life was spent in the printing trade. In 1988 he published an entertaining memoir of his football career, "Playing for Fun".

FISHER, Frederick William

(Millwall and the Royal Air Force)
(1 England wartime app.)

Born: Dodworth, Barnsley, 11 Apr. 1910
Killed in action over Europe, Sep. 1944
1938: 5-5, 10-7
Career: Monckton Athletic; Barnsley Nov. 1933; Chesterfield Feb. 1938 (£500); Millwall Nov. 1938 (£1600)

Outside-right neatly summed up in a 1938 annual as "...a bundle of energy and a game fighter". Small physically but that did not prevent an ability to also play centre-forward. Had an eye for a scoring chance, slotting in 4 against Bradford in a 1935/36 encounter. In 1938 represented the Central League against the London Combination. Lost his life while serving as a rear gunner.

FLEWIN, Reginald

(Portsmouth and the Royal Navy)
(1 England wartime app.)

Born: Portsmouth, 28 Nov. 1920
1949: 5-11½, 13-0
Career: Ryde Sports (Isle of Wight); Portsmouth on amateur forms before signing as a prof. Nov. 1937 - 1953 then serving as the club's coach and assistant manager until his appointment as Stockport County manager Sep. 1960; Bournemouth & Boscombe Athletic manager July 1963 - Nov. 1965, resigning on health grounds; Hastings United manager 1967 - 1968. Afterwards employed as manager of a holiday camp in Ventnor, IOW.

Other Honours: (Portsmouth) FL champions 1949, 1950.

Centre-half. 'Sheet anchor' and skipper of the fine Pompey side that won the League title in successive seasons. Reg, outstanding in defence, maintained a long club tradition of notable pivots with, as one writer put it, "stamina to match his 13 stone frame". He was flanked by international wing-halves in the two Jimmys - Scoular and Dickinson. Team manager of the FA touring parties to Canada (1950) and Australia (1951).

FRANKLIN, Cornelius ("Neil")
(Stoke City and the Royal Air Force)
(10 England wartime apps.)
Born: Stoke-on-Trent, 24 Jan. 1922
1949: 5-11, 11-1

Career: Potteries schoolboy football; Stoke Old Boys; Stoke City ground staff 1936, turning prof. Jan. 1939; Santa Fe, Bogota May 1950; Hull City Feb. 1951 (£22,500); Crewe Alexandra Feb. 1956 (£1250); Stockport County Oct. 1957 (£1250); Wellington Town as player/coach July 1959; Sankey's FC (Wellington, Salop) July 1960, as player/manager for 1960/61 season, retiring Dec. 1962. Coach to Appoel FC, Nicosia, Feb. 1963; Colchester United manager Nov. 1963 - May 1968. Later an Oswaldtwistle licensee.

Other Honours: England (27 'full' apps.)
England 'B' international (1 app.)
Football League (5 apps.)

Centre-half, the king-pin of the berth in the immediate post-war years. Master of all pivotal aspects; posi

---

tioning, heading, tackling, distribution, controlling his defence and never yielding. It seems strange this brilliant player acquired no club honours.

GIBBONS, Albert Henry ("Jack")
(Tottenham Hotspur and the Royal Air Force)
(1 England wartime app.)
Born: Fulham, London, 10 Apr. 1914
1949: 5-9, 11-5

Career: Represented the RAF while serving as a regular in the 1930's when he also assisted Uxbridge, Hayes and Kingstonian before signing amateur forms for Tottenham Hotspur in July 1937 and Brentford Aug. 1938. Re-joined Tottenham as a prof. Aug. 1939. Transferred to Bradford May 1946 and Brentford again Aug. 1947 (£10,000), retiring May 1949 and becoming the Bees' secretary/manager to Aug. 1952. Subsequently coached all over the world, including Belgium, Israel, Australia and South Africa.

Other Honours: England amateur international (6 apps.)
FA touring party to South Africa 1939, twice appearing against the South African national side.
Middlesex County when an amateur during the 1930's.

Centre/inside-forward, one of the crack amateurs of the 'thirties. Especially noted for his goal scoring aptitude which continued after joining the paid ranks. Strong in all aspects of attacking play whether ground or aerial.

GOSLIN, Henry A.
(Bolton Wanderers and The Army)
(4 England wartime apps.)
Born: Willington, Derbyshire, 9 Nov. 1909
Killed in action, 18 Dec. 1943
1938: 5-11¼, 11-2½
Career: Nottingham schools and Boys' Brigade football; Boots Athletic (Nottingham); Bolton Wanderers Apr. 1930 to his death.

Right-half who also appeared at centre-half and, in an emergency, full-back. Derbyshire born, he was brought up in Nottingham, hence the schoolboy and Boots Athletic connection - he worked for the Boots company. Quickly winning a first team place, he skippered Bolton from the mid- 'thirties, making in all

334 League and FA cup appearances. *Harry was a commanding figure, skilled in all half-back arts. Called up immediately on the outbreak of war - he had been a Territorial for 4 years - he served in the Royal Artillery in France and Africa before losing his life in Italy. A wartime guest for Norwich City and Chelsea. Had a cycle shop in Bolton.*

GOULDEN, Leonard Arthur
(West Ham United)
(6 England wartime apps., 3 goals)
Born: Hackney, London, 16 July 1912
Died: 14 Feb. 1995
1938: 5-8, 10-12
Career: West Ham Schools; West Ham United amateur 1931, gaining experience with Chelmsford and Leyton before signing as a prof. Apr. 1933; Chelsea Dec. 1945 (£5000), retired cs 1950 and joined that club's training staff; Watford manager (including spell as general manager) Nov. 1952 - July 1956; Watford coach July 1959 - May 1962; later coach in Libya for 2 years; Manager Banbury United Mar. 1967; Oxford Utd. trainer/coach Jan.1969 for a spell.

Other Honours: England schoolboy international (2 apps.)
Football League (2 apps.)

Inside-left. Very prominent in the 1930's when his brainy play was at its peak. A feature was the ability to change a point of attack to telling effect. His son, Roy, also gained England schoolboy international honours. Len's activities outside football have included working as a postmaster and at a USAF base in Northants.

GREENHALGH, Norman H.
(Everton)
(1 England wartime app.)

Born: Bolton, 10 Aug. 1914
1938: 5-10, 11-8
Career: Local junior football to Bolton Wanderers on amateur forms May 1935, turning prof. the following Aug.; New Brighton Oct. 1935; Everton Jan. 1938; Bangor City cs 1950.

Other Honours: Football League (1 app.)
(Everton) FL champions 1939

Left-back, a doughty ever-present in Everton's 1938/9 championship line-up, forming a stout and effective full-back partnership with the Irish international, Willie Cook. Norman had played in several other positions before finding his true vocation. After his football days employed as a licensee. His son, David, assisted (by then, non-League) New Brighton in the '70's.

HAGAN, James
(Sheffield United and The Army)
(16 England wartime apps., 13 goals)

Born: Washington, Co. Durham, 21 Jan. 1918
1949: 5-8, 10-10
Career: Washington Schools (Liverpool on amateur forms Jan. 1932); Derby County amateur cs 1933, turning prof. for that club Jan. 1935; Sheffield United Nov. 1938 (£2500); retired Mar. 1958; Peterborough United manager Aug. 1958 - Oct. 1962; West Bromwich Albion manager Apr. 1963 - May 1967; Manchester City scout 1967-68; Benfica (Portugal) manager/trainer Mar. 1970 - Sep. 1973; coach in Kuwait 1974-76, later in 1976 starting a spell as manager Sporting Club de Portugal (Lisbon)

In the mid- 'thirties Jimmy was hailed by the great Steve Bloomer as a major find, early giving evidence of subtlety and tactical awareness, extremely unusual for one in his mid-teens. Frequent England wartime appearances were followed by only one 'full' cap, which seems scant reward, but he was a contemporary of Carter, Mannion and Mortensen. Son of Alf Hagan who assisted Newcastle, Cardiff and Tranmere Rovers in the decade immediately following the 1914/18 war.

HALL, G(eorge) William
(Tottenham Hotspur)
(3 England wartime apps.)

Born: Newark, Notts., 12 Mar. 1912
Died: 22 May 1967
1938: 5-6½, 11-9
Career: Notts Schools; Ransome & Marles FC (Newark); Notts County Nov. 1930; Tottenham Hotspur Dec. 1932 (for a fee that subsequently attracted a further £500 for his initial England appearance); retired through injury 1944. Clapton Orient manager/coach Sep. 1945, resigned on health grounds two months later. Subsequently had a brief spell from Dec. 1949 as Chingford Town's manager.

Other Honours: England (10 'full' apps.)
Football League (3 apps.)

Inside-forward possessing fine ball control and dribbling skills who made history by scoring 5 goals in succession against Northern Ireland in Nov. 1938, the first 3 of which were netted in 3½ minutes. Became seriously ill with thrombosis in 1945, eventually having both legs amputated. Nonetheless in his last years

Willie had spells as partner in a sports outfitting business and as the landlord of an Aldgate (London) hostelry.

HANSON, Adolphe Jonathan ("Alf")
(Chelsea)
(1 England wartime app.)
Born: Bootle, 27 Feb. 1912
1938: 5-8½, 10-10

Career: Bootle JOC (during which period he assisted Everton 'A'); Liverpool Nov. 1931; Chelsea July 1938 (£7500); South Liverpool

player/manager 1945; Shelbourne player/manager 1946; subsequently player/manager of Ellermere Port Town from Feb. 1949.

Outside-left. A no-nonsense performer whose chief qualities of speed and directness were utilised to good effect. His aggregate career figures reflect this; 220 League and FA Cup outings for Liverpool and Chelsea in which he notched 61 goals - an excellent haul for a wingman. The Second World War obviously robbed Alf of some plum seasons. Elder brother of the long-serving (1935-1956) Bolton Wanderers goalkeeper, Stan Hanson.

HAPGOOD, Edris Albert
(Arsenal and the Royal Air Force)
(13 England wartime apps.)
Born: Bristol, 24 Sep. 1908
Died: 20 Apr. 1973
1938: 5-8½, 10-8
Career: Bristol junior football (Bristol Rovers amateur 1926); Kettering Town cs 1927; Arsenal Oct. 1927 (£750); retired 1944; Blackburn Rovers manager June 1946 - Feb. 1947; Shrewsbury Town player/coach Aug. 1947; Watford manager Feb. 1948; Bath City manager Mar. 1950 - Feb. 1956.

Other Honours: England (30 'full' apps.)
Football League (4 apps.)
(Arsenal) FL champions 1931, 1933, 1934, 1935, 1938
FA Cup winner 1930, 1936; finalist 1932.

Left-back. England have been extraordinarily well served in this position down the years. Eddie Hapgood

was a prominent member of the cavalcade, an outstanding successor to the great Ernie Blenkinsop. He resembled Blenkinsop in style with respect to calculated tackles and clearances and general polish. On leaving football worked as a Youth Hostel warden, later retiring to Leamington Spa.

HARDWICK, George Francis M.
(Middlesbrough and the Royal Air Force)
(17 England wartime apps.)
Born: Saltburn, Yorks., 2 Feb. 1920
1949: 5-9½, 12-0
Career: Cleveland schools football; South Bank East End 1934; Middlesbrough on amateur forms Oct. 1935, turning prof. Apr. 1937; Oldham Athletic as player/manager Nov. 1950 (£15,000) - Apr. 1956 when he resigned and also retired from playing; coach to US Army team in Suttgart, Germany, Aug. 1956; Eindhoven FC (Holland) coach June 1957 for 2 years; Middlesbrough youth team coach Aug. 1961 - Nov. 1963; Sunderland Manager Nov. 1964 - May 1965; Gateshead manager 1968 - Feb. 1970.

Other Honours: England (13 'full' apps.)
Great Britain (vs. Rest of Europe, 1947)
Football League (3 apps.)
(Oldham) FL Div.3 (North) champions 1953

Left-back. One who came to the fore in wartime following a brief introduction to the League game in season 1937/38. Both cultured and ultra-reliable, Hardwick skippered England in all his post-war appearances and also Great Britain in the 1947 encounter. Played in attack at school and during the Oldham Athletic spell. Outside the game he worked at

different times in garage management and the steel industry.

HARPER, Bernard
(Barnsley)
(1 England wartime app.)
Born: Gawber, Barnsley, 23 Nov. 1912
1938: 5-11, 13-7
Career: Barugh Green; Barnsley Aug. 1932 (originally on trial); Scunthorpe United player/manager 1946 - 1948.

Other Honours: (Barnsley) FL Div.3 (North) champions 1934, 1939

Right/centre-half. Secured from local junior soccer, Harper turned out to be one of the Colliers' best interwar signings. He made his senior debut in Jan. 1933 and from then until his final appearance (29 Apr. 1939) played 228 League and FA Cup matches. Blessed with a handy physique, he was equally effective at wing-half or as pivot and captained the side to promotion in 1938/39.

JOHNSON, W(illiam) Herbert
(Charlton Athletic and the Royal Air Force)
(2 England wartime apps.)
Born: Stockton-on-Tees, 4 June 1916
1949: 5-7½, 10-9
Career: Stockton schools; Norton Juniors; South Bank; Stockton FC; Spennymoor United; Charlton Athletic Mar. 1939 (£400); Bexleyheath & Welling player/manager July 1953; Cambridge

United player/manager Nov. 1955; Leicester City chief scout June 1959, subsequently serving as that club's assistant manager and chief coach; later scouted for Nottingham Forest, Derby County and Southampton, and finally on Walsall's staff before retiring in the 1981 close season.

Other Honours: (Charlton) FA Cup winner 1947; finalist 1946.

Wing-half. In his many guest appearances for Bolton Wanderers during the war, he developed into a skilful, thoughtful half. So much so Bolton were desirous of engaging him permanently. Like several of his Charl-ton era, both long-serving and this service with but one League club. One good judge reckoned Johnson would have been equally good at inside-forward.

JOY, Bernard
(Arsenal and the Royal Air Force)
(1 England wartime app.)
Born: Fulham, London, 29 Oct. 1911
Died: 18 July 1984
1938: 6-1, 12-6
Career: London University; Casuals, during which period he was on the books of Southend United and Fulham as an amateur; Corinthians in the mid-1930's; Arsenal May 1935 - cs 1947 when he rejoined Casuals, retiring a year later.

Other Honours: England (1 'full' app.)
England amateur international (12 apps.)
(Casuals) FA Amateur Cup winner 1936
(Arsenal) FL champions 1938

Centre-half. An amateur of the highest class, a fact proven by his ability to succeed Herbie Roberts in the Arsenal line-up. Joy, in fact, resembled Roberts with his 'third back' style, concentrating on defence. Worked initially as a schoolmaster later becoming a football corresopndent with the London papers, "Star" and "Evening Standard", retiring Oct. 1976. He also wrote an excellent club history, "Forward Arsenal !", published by Phoenix House in 1952.

KINSELL, T(homas) Henry
(West Bromwich Albion and The Army)
(2 England wartime apps.)
Born: Cannock, Staffs., 31 May 1921
1949: 5-11, 12-8
Career: Cannock schools football; West Bromwich Albion staff May 1935, turning prof. June 1938; Bolton Wanderers June 1949 (£12,000, a then Bolton record); Reading May 1950; West Ham United Jan. 1951; Bedford Town July 1956; retired 1957.

Other Honour: Junior internationalist 1939

Left-back. A fine back, quick moving and one to use his brains. Exploited the overlapping maneouvre to some purpose. Being a contemporary of George Hardwick doubtless robbed him of full England selection. Harry guested for Blackpool, Grimsby Town and Middlesbrough and assisted the FA Services XI against Switzerland in 1945.

Outside-right with an unusually hefty physique for the berth, a fact unsettling to opposing defenders. Alf also possessed speed and scoring ability, almost averaging a goal every two games. Served as a P.T. Instructor in the wartime RAF, during which time a bad knee injury ended his playing career. Later a Norfolk farmer, retiring in 1980. Also represented England at clay-pigeon shooting.

LAWTON, Thomas

(Everton, Chelsea and The Army)
(23 England wartime apps., 24 goals)
Born: Bolton, 6 Oct. 1919
1947: 5-11, 12-0
Career: Bolton schools football; Lancashire Schools; Hayes Athletic; Rossendale United when 15, at which time he had signed amateur forms for Bolton Wanderers and Sheffield Wednesday; Burnley as an amateur May 1935, signing as a prof. Oct. 1936; Everton Jan. 1937 (£6,500); Chelsea Nov. 1945 (£11,500); Notts County Nov. 1947 (£20,000 and another player); Brentford Mar. 1952 (£12,000) (player/manager from Jan. 1953); Arsenal Sep. 1953 (£10,000 and another player); Kettering Town player/manager Feb. 1956 (£1,000) - Apr. 1957; Notts County manager May 1957 - July 1958; Kettering Town manager Nov. 1963; Apr. 1964 appointed director; Notts. County coach and chief scout Oct. 1968 - Apr. 1970.

Other Honours: England (23 'full' apps.)
Football League (3 apps.)
(Everton) FL champions 1939
(Notts County) FL Div.3 (South) champions 1950

KIRCHEN, Alfred John

(Arsenal and the Royal Air Force)
(3 England wartime apps.)
Born: Shouldham, Norfolk, 26 Apr. 1913
1938: 5-11½, 12-1
Career: King's Lynn Schools; Norfolk Schools; King's Lynn Old Boys; Shouldham FC; Norwich City on amateur forms Oct. 1933, turning prof. a month later; Arsenal Mar. 1935 (£6,000); retired through injury 1943; had short spell as Norwich City trainer 1946 and was later a director of that club.

Other Honours: England (3 'full' apps.)
(Arsenal) FL champions 1938

Centre-forward to be numbered among the greatest of modern times. Tommy had all the attributes in head-work and footwook, distribution and awareness as to

the creation of goals whether for team-mates or personally. The fact he suffered from flat feet mattered nothing. His extraordinary promise when a youngster was completely realised. He became the youngest player to register a League hat-trick : 4 days after his 17th birthday!

LEWIS, James William
(Walthamstow Avenue)
(1 England wartime app. as a substitute)
Born: Hackney, London, 21 Dec. 1905
Died: Mar. 1976
1930's: 5-9, 12-0
Career: London junior football to Walthamstow Avenue 1929; Queen's Park Rangers 1931 - 1932; Walthamstow Avenue again cs 1932, retired during the War.

Other Honours: England amateur international (13 apps.)
Member of FA touring party to South Africa 1939, twice playing against that country's national side.

Inside-right able to take the right-half berth. One of the most distringuished amateurs of his time, which was the decade preceding the Second World War. Sound in all aspects of wing-half and inside-forward play, able in combination and with the ability to seize a scoring opportunity himself. Made 13 League appearances, scoring 4 goals, in his year with Queen's Park Rangers. Father of J.L. Lewis of Chelsea's 1954/5 League championship side who, like his father, remained an amateur throughout his career and won

England amateur honours. Lewis' appearance in a 1940 wartime international was the first substitution in a British big match, so consequently ranks as a 'feat' for the player that was, and is, unique.

MANNION, Wilfred J.
(Middlesbrough and The Army)
(4 England wartime apps.)
Born: South Bank, Middlesbrough, 16 May 1918
1950: 5-5, 11-0
Career: South Bank St. Peter's; Middlesbrough on amateur forms Sep. 1936, turing prof. Jan. 1937; retired June 1954 but joined Hull City the following Dec. (£5,000); Poole Town Sep. 1955 - Mar. 1956; Cambridge United Aug. 1956; King's Lynn May 1958; Haverhill Rovers (Suffolk) Oct. 1958 - cs 1959; Earlestown (Lancashire Combination) as player/manager Oct. 1962.

Other Honours: England (26 'full' apps.)
England "B" international (3 apps.)
Football League (7 apps.)

Inside-forward nicknamed "the Golden Boy of Soccer", in part for his blond locks but chiefly for outstanding skill. Wilf played an orthodox game but his orthodoxy, especially in the matter of ball control and distribution, was of a standard reached by few. He returned to live on his native Teeside after the Earleston engagement.

MAPSON, John

(Sunderland)

(1 England wartime app.)

Born: Birkenhead, 2 May 1917

1950: 5-11¾, 13-0

Career: Swindon Schools; Highworth FC (Wilts.) (signed amateur form for Swindon Town when 16); Guildford City; Reading Apr. 1935 (returned to Guildford on loan for part of season 1935/6); Sunderland Mar. 1936 (£1,000); retired cs 1954.

Other Honours: FA tourist to South Africa 1939 (played in 2 Tests) (Sunderland) FA Cup winner 1937

Goalkeeper. Moved to Swindon when a child, hence an early career spent in the South. His all round competence brought a rapid rise. With only a couple of League outings under his belt John was signed by Sunderland, still under 19, to succeed the later Jimmy Thorpe. It was a shrewd signing, John making 345 peacetime League appearances for the Wearsiders before retiring at 37. He subsequently worked in the furniture and upholstery trade. During the War he was employed in a Royal Ordnance engineering factory.

MARKS, W(illiam) George

(Arsenal and the Royal Air Force)

(8 England wartime apps.)

Born: Figheldean, nr. Amesbury, Wilts., 9 Apr. 1915

1950: 5-11½, 12-12

Career: Salisbury Corinthians; Arsenal amateur Mar. 1936, prof. May 1936, subsequently developing with their nursery side, Margate, and returning to Highbury May 1938; Blackburn Rovers Aug. 1946 (£5,000); Bristol City Aug. 1948; Reading Oct. 1948; retired Apr. 1954 and worked on that club's training staff until 1955. As a reinstated amateur he assisted a Wiltshire junior club, Bulford United, 1955-56.

Goalkeeper. A fine custodian, brisk and sure in action and quite reliable. As will be realised by the number of his wartime England appearances, Marks came to his peak during those years. Although he attracted a then appreciable fee on the return to peacetime soccer, he was then 31. After 2 years at Ewood Park he moved down a couple of Divisions to spend the remainder of his playing career in the Southern Section.

MARTIN, John Rowland

(Aston Villa and The Army)

(2 England wartime apps., 1 goal)

Born: Hamstead, Birmingham, 5 Aug. 1914

1939: 5-10, 11-4

Career: Hednesdford Town; Aston Villa on amateur forms Oct. 1934, turning prof. 1935; returned to Hednesford Town in the close season of 1949, later acting as that club's manager for a time.

Inside-right/centre-forward, lively and enthusiastice whose style was succinctly (and accurately) summed up in one quarter as 'Corinthian'. Broke into Villa's first team in the season before the War. Due to the conflict, his aggregate League and FA Cup appearances total was but 53. However, a goals total of 22 illus-

trates Martin's eye for a scoring opportunity.   A schoolmaster by calling, he was latterly a headmaster.

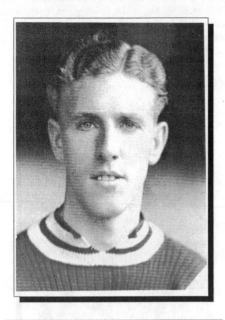

MASON, George William
(Coventry City)
(2 England wartime apps.)
Born: Birmingham, 5 Sep. 1913
Died: 12 Aug. 1993
1938: 6-0, 12-1½
Career: South Birmingham Schools; Redhill Amateurs (Staffs.); Coventry City Nov. 1931; Nuneaton Borough cs 1952; retired Sep. 1953 but signed for Bedworth Town cs 1954 for a brief spell.

Other Honours: England schoolboy international (1 app.)
(Coventry City) FL Div.3 (South) champions 1936

Centre-half. One of the greatest-ever clubmen, his service to Coventry City extending over 20 years and their skipper for most of that long period. George was in the sheet anchor mould, dominating and marshalling fellow defenders. He would surely have won 'full' caps but for the War. Mason purchased a public house in 1952 and was a licensee for much of the remainder of his working life. He also worked for Jaguar. One of his sons, John, became an England amateur international who later played professionally for Peterborough United.

MATTHEWS, (Sir) Stanley
(Stoke City and the Royal Air Force)
(29 England wartime apps., 2 goals)
Born: Hanley, Stoke-on-Trent, 1 Feb. 1915
1938: 5-9, 10-10
Career: Hanley Schools; Stoke St. Peter's; Stoke City amateur Sep. 1930, prof. Feb. 1932; Blackpool May 1947 (£11,500); Stoke City again Oct. 1961 (£2,500); retired 1965. Port Vale general manager July 1965 - July 1968 subsequently acting in an honorary advisory capacity; Hibernian FC (Malta) manager Apr. 1970; coach in Soweta, South Africa 1974-76.

Other Honours: England (54 'full' apps.)
Football League (13 apps.)
England schoolboy international
(Stoke City) FL Div.2 champions 1933, 1963
(Blackpool) FA Cup winner 1953, finalist 1948, 1951

Outside-right. One of the greatest footballers produced in Britain - or anywhere else for that matter.

Forever remembered by anyone priviledged to see him in action with his wizardry in the dribble, his swerves, side-steps and numerous other tricks deluding the best of opposing defenders. Awarded the CBE in 1957, knighted in 1965 - the first footballer to receive these high honours - and awarded an honorary degree at Keele University in 1987. Twice the Football Writers' "Player of the Year" (1948 and 1963).

MERCER, Joseph
(Everton and The Army)
(27 England wartime apps., 1 goal)

Born: 9 Aug. 1914
Died: 9 Aug. 1990 (his 76th birthday)
1939: 5-9, 11-0

Career: Ellesmere Port Schools; Cheshire Schools; Elton Green FC (Ince); Shell-Mex FC (Liverpool County Combination); Ellesmere Port Town (during which spell he played a few games with Runcorn); Everton on amateur forms during season 1931/32, turning prof. Sep. 1932; Arsenal Nov. 1946 (£7,000); retired through injury cs 1955. Sheffield United Manager Aug. 1955; Aston Villa manager Dec. 1958 - July 1964; Manchester City manager July 1965 and general manager from Oct. 1971; Coventry City general manager June 1972 and then serving as a director Apr. 1975 - July 1981.

Other Honours: England (5 'full' apps.)
Football League (1 app.)
(Everton) FL champions 1939
Arsenal FL champions 1948, 1953
FA Cup winner 1950, finalist 1952

Wing-half. A leading personality from the 'thirties onwards and hugely popular everywhere with his

happy disposition. Joe's spindly legs became famous and the cartoonists' delight. His telling tackling was allied to attacking instincts that almost made him a sixth forward. Retired through injury (the double fracture of a leg), at 41! Prominent in the managerial field subsequently.

MORTENSEN, Stanley Harding
(Blackpool and the Royal Air Force)
(3 England wartime apps., 3 goals)

Born: South Shields, 26 May 1921
Died: 22 May 1991
1950: 5-9½, 11-7

Career: After schools football joined South Shields Ex-Schoolboys FC from whom he joined Blackpool in Apr. 1937; Hull City Nov. 1955 (£2,000); Southport Feb. 1957; Bath City July 1958; retired in May 1959 but signed for Lancaster City Nov. 1960, finally retiring Mar. 1962. Blackpool manager Feb. 1967 - Apr. 1969

Other Honours: England (25 'full' apps.)
England 'B' international (1 app.)
Football League (5 apps.)
(Blackpool) FA Cup winner 1953, finalist 1948, 1951

Centre/inside-forward. No senior appearances pre-war but made a considerable name before peace returned and was a major personality of the immediate post-war years. Renowned for electrifying bursts of speed, marksmanship and the heights he was able to achieve when heading the ball. Morty had the unique experience of appearing for Wales as a substitute in a wartime international. Served as an Air Force bomber pilot, a bad crash fortunately not affecting his footballing career. Later a Blackpool business man.

MOUNTFORD, Reginald Charles
(Huddersfield Town and the Royal Air Force)
(1 England wartime app.)

Born: Darlington, 1908
1938: 5-9, 11-3

Career: Darlington schools and junior football; Darlington FC amateur during season 1928/29; Huddersfield Town as a prof. May 1929; retired before the ending of WW2. Coach to Combinag FC, Copenhagen, May 1946, later coaching the Danish national side for the 1948 Olympic Games.

Other Honour: (Huddersfield) FA Cup finalist 1938

Left-back. Developed his game in his native Darlington while working as a miner. As a full time Huddersfield player he eventually emerged as a top flight defender both sound and resourceful. This was in 1935/36 with 75 Division 1 appearances under his belt from previous campaigns. Mountford assisted half a dozen clubs during the War including three in the London area : Brentford, Chelsea and Palace.

MULLEN, James
(Wolverhampton Wanderers and The Army)
(3 England wartime apps.)

Born: Newcastle-upon-Tyne, 6 Jan. 1923
Died: 13 Oct. 1987
1939: 5-9½, 11-0

Career: Newcastle Schools; Wolverhampton Wanderers' ground staff July 1937, turning prof. Jan. 1940; retired cs 1960.

Other Honours: England (12 'full' apps.)
England 'B' (3 apps.)

England schoolboy international (1 app.)
Football League (1 app.)
(Wolves) FL champions 1954, 1958, 1959
FA Cup winner 1949

Outside-left, notable for a very early, successful introduction into the 'big time'. Made his First Division debut at 16 and played in an FA Cup semi-final at the same age, being, in all probability, the youngest ever to appear in the competition's penultimate stage. Jimmy was heftily built for a wingman and possessed marksmanship that he demonstrated on cutting-in from the touch-line. Latterly a sports shop owner in Wolverhampton.

OAKES, John
(Charlton Athletic and the Royal Air Force)
(1 England wartime app.)

Born: Winsford, Cheshire, 13 Sep. 1905
Died: 20 Mar. 1992
1949: 5-10, 12-0

Career: Cargo Fleet & Cockrane's FC (South Bank League); Nottingham Forest Aug. 1928; Crook Town cs 1930; Southend United May 1931; Crook Town again cs 1932; Spennymoor United Feb. 1933; Aldershot Aug. 1934; Charlton Athletic Mar. 1936 (£650); Plymouth Argyle July 1947; Snowdon Colliery Welfare player/manager July 1949 - Feb. 1953; Gravesend & Northfleet trainer July 1953, later a coach in Sweden for some years.

Other Honours: (Charlton) FA Cup finalist 1946
He represented England against South Africa in 1939 but this did not rank as a 'full' international.

Centre-half. An extraordinary career in that he twice left the League scene to return when nearly 29, established himself as a leading pivot and remained a League player until the ripe age of 44. Strong defensively - a real 'sheet anchor'. Worked in a Kent paper mill before going to live in the States and, later Australia, where he died in Perth in his 87th year. Quite possibly the oldest player to have appeared in an FA Cup final.

PEARSON, Thomas Usher
(Newcastle United and the Royal Air Force)
(1 England wartime app.)
Born: Edinburgh, 6 Mar. 1913
1938: 5-7½, 10-2
Career: Murrayfield Amateurs (Edinburgh); Newcastle United Mar. 1933 (£35); Aberdeen Feb. 1948 (in exchange for another player); retired 1953; thereupon became a sports journalist and coach to Aberdeen FC juniors; Aberdeen manager Nov. 1959 - Feb. 1965; Newcastle United's Scottish scout (based in Edinburgh) for a period from June 1967.

Other Honours: Scotland (2 apps.)
Scottish League (1 app.)

Outside-left. A unique case : a Scot turning out for England! It happened because the selected left-winger was injured in a car accident en route to the match, which was to take place at Newcastle's St. James Park. Pearson was a rare handful for any opposing winghalf. He possessed speed and ball control, and was as tricky as they come and a proven goalscorer.

PYE, Jesse
(Notts County and The Army)
(1 England wartime app., 1 goal)
Born: Treeton, nr. Rotherham, 22 Dec. 1918
Died: 20 Feb. 1984
1949: 5-10, 11-9
Career: Catliffe Boys Club; Treeton Rovers; Sheffield United amateur 1938, later becoming a part-time prof.; Notts County Aug. 1945; Wolverhampton Wanderers May 1946 (£10,000); Luton Town July 1952 (£9,000+); Derby County Oct. 1954 (c. £5,000); Wisbech Town July 1957, becoming player/manager Mar. 1960, resigning the managership 1966.

Other Honours: England (1 'full' app.)
England 'B' (3 apps.)
Football League (1 app.)
(Wolves) FA Cup winner 1949

Centre/Inside-forward. Captivated onlookers home and away with his elegant skills that were a fetching amalgam of craft and penetration. His League record reads 145 goals in 209 appearances - an excellent return. After leaving football was the proprietor of a Blackpool hotel.

RICHARDSON, Joseph
(Newcastle United and the National Fire Service)
(1 England wartime app.)
Born: Bedlington, Northumberland, 24 Aug. 1908
Died: 1977
1938: 5-8, 11-9
Career: New Delaval Villa; Blyth Spartans; Newcastle United Apr. 1929 (£250 including another player); retired during WW2 to become Newcastle's assistant trainer for the remainder of his life.

Right-back. A real Geordie loyalist : a supporter before going to St. James Park and remaining there nearly half a century. Joe didn't stand on ceremony as a player, defending doggedly, clearing the ball quickly utilising a long clearance. Sure of foot and possessing lots of stamina.

ROOKE, Ronald Leslie
(Fulham and the Royal Air Force)
(1 England wartime app.)
Born: Guildford, Surrey, 7 Dec. 1912
Died: 9 June 1985
1938: 5-9, 12-4
Career: Guildford junior football (trial with Stoke City); Woking; Guildford City; Crystal Palace Mar. 1933; Fulham Oct. 1936; Arsenal Dec. 1946 (£1,000 and 2 players); Crystal Palace again (as player/manager) June 1949, retired from playing 1950 and resigned managership Dec. 1950; Bedford Town player/manager Feb. 1951. Second spell managing Bedford Town from 1959 close season.

Other Honour: (Arsenal) FL champions 1948

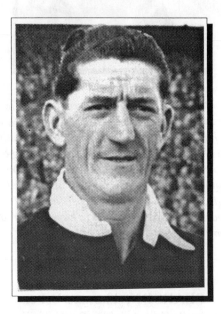

Centre/inside-forward. A long career with its peacetime highlight, a League championship medal, coming in his 37th year. That move to Highbury was surprising at the time, a veteran from a lower Division, but well justified in the event. Rooke fitted in admirably with fellow inside-forwards Reg Lewis and Jimmy Logie. He was extremely powerful physically, a noted goalscorer, strong in both feet, and topped the League scoring list in that memorable 1947/8 campaign.

ROWLEY, John Frederick
(Manchester United and The Army)
(1 England wartime app.)
Born: Wolverhampton, 7 Oct. 1920
1938: 5-9, 11-7
Career: Dudley Old Boys; Wolverhampton Wanderers Nov. 1935 (on loan to Cradley Heath Oct. 1936, plus Bournemouth & Bos. Ath. Feb. 1937); Manchester United Oct. 1937 (£3,500); Plymouth Argyle

as player/manager Feb. 1955 retiring from playing cs 1957 and remaining as manager until Mar. 1960; Oldham Athletic manager July 1960 - July 1963; Ajax FC (Amsterdam) coach Aug. 1963 - July 1964; Wrexham manager Jan. 1966; Bradford general manager Apr. 1967; Oldham Athletic manager again Oct. 1968 - Dec. 1969.

Other Honours: England (6 'full' apps.)
England 'B' (1 app.)
Football League (2 apps.)
(Manchester Utd) FL champions 1952
FA Cup winner 1948

Forward, famously versatile; in his half-dozen England outings four different attack positions were occupied, outside-right being the only missing one. A naturally lively and aggressive performer, Jack carried an especially searing shot that led to him getting the label of "The Gunner". Older brother of Arthur Rowley (Leicester City and England 'B').

ROXBURGH, Alexander White
(Blackpool and the National Fire Service)
(1 England wartime app.)
Born: Manchester, 19 Sep. 1910
Died: 5 Dec. 1985
1938: 6-1¾, 11-6
Career: Blackpool junior football (Manchester City amateur); Blackpool FC Jan. 1931 on amateur forms, later that season joining the prof. staff; Barrow Aug. 1946; Hyde United 1948.

Goalkeeper. Pre-war - thanks to the presence of the excellent Jock Wallace - he enjoyed but one season (1937/38) when he clocked up over half the possible

League appearances. Nevertheless, Roxburgh was a useful 'keeper to have on the books with his rangy build and long reach. Some sources claim he was discovered keeping goal in a Blackpool fairground booth - a real boys' magazine fiction situation if ever there was one!

SCOTT, Laurence
(Arsenal and the Royal Air Force)
(16 England wartime apps.)
Born: Sheffield, 23 Apr. 1917
1949: 5-9½, 11-8

Career: Sheffield Schools; Edgar Allen's FC (Sheffield); Bradford City amateur as early as 1931, turning prof. May 1935; Arsenal Feb. 1937 (in exchange for another player); Crystal Palace player/manager Oct. 1951, retiring from playing Aug. 1953 and continuing as manager to Sep. 1954; Hendon FC manager later that season until the summer of 1957; Hitchin Town manager for a spell from Aug. 1957.

Other Honours: England (17 'full' apps.)
England 'B' (4 apps.)
Football League (5 apps.)
(Arsenal) FL champions 1948
FA Cup winner 1950

Right-back of all round skills with his strong tackling, thoughtful, positioning, and admirably placed clearances. Additionally he was fast moving, indeed he was reckoned the speediest full-back of his time. Scott served as a PT Instructor during the War. After leaving football worked as a hardware firm's sales representative until retirement.

SHACKLETON, Leonard Francis
(Bradford)
(1 England wartime app.)
Born: Bradford, 3 May 1922
1950: 5-7½, 11-5
Career: Bradford Schools; Kippax United; Arsenal ground staff Aug. 1938 (loaned for development to London Paper Mills and Enfield) returning home when War broke out; Bradford as a prof. Dec. 1940 (Bradford City guest player during WW2); Newcastle United Oct. 1946 (£13,000); Sunderland Feb. 1948 (£20,050), retiring through injury Sep. 1957.

Other Honours: England (5 'full' apps.)
England 'B' (2 apps.)
England schoolboy international (3 apps.)
Football League (2 apps.)

Inside-forward celebrated for his ball manipulation and trickery, delighting spectators for a decade after the War's end. There has probably never been a more brilliant player of this type. Nicknamed 'The Clown Prince of Soccer' this was also the title of his book, an irreverent work that caused a sensation. A good cricketer, Len played occasionally for Northumberland in the Minor Counties. Later a North-East sports journalist and, from 1976, a director of Fulham FC for a time.

SMITH, George Casper
(Charlton Athletic and The Army)
(1 England wartime app.)
Born: Poplar, London, 23 Apr. 1915
Died: 31 Oct. 1983
1939: 6-1½, 12-2
Career: Hackney Schools; Army football; Bexleyheath & Welling 1937/38 season; Charlton Athletic Aug. 1938; Brentford Nov. 1945 (£3,000); Queen's Park Rangers May 1947; Ipswich Town as player/assistant manager Apr. - Dec. 1949; Chelmsford City Aug. 1950; Redhill manager/coach July 1951; Eastbourne United manager/coach 1952/55, also at this time coach to the FA Youth side; Sheffield United coach Sep. 1955; Sutton United mananger/coach May 1956; Crystal Palace manager June 1958; Sheffield United chief coach Apr. 1960; Portsmouth manager Mar. 1961 - Mar. 1970.

Other Honour: (QPR) FL Div.3 (South) champions 1948

Centre-half with the physical attributes necessary for the defensive role the position demanded in his day. Smith had originally been a schoolboy goalkeeper but had moved to pivot before becoming a Bexleyheath & Welling professional. Joining up in 1939, he played representative football for both The Army and the Combined Services before the end of WW2. Skippered Queen's Park Rangers to their 1948 promotion triumph.

SMITH, J(ames) C(hristopher) Reginald
(Millwall and the Wartime Police Force)
(3 England wartime apps.)
Born: Battersea, London, 20 Jan. 1912
1938: 5-9, 11-8
Career: Hitchin Town (Tottenham Hotspur amateur cs 1932); Millwall as a prof. Aug. 1935; Dundee Mar. 1946; Corby Town player/manager 1948; Dundee trainer/coach early in 1949; Dundee United manager Sep. 1954; Falkirk manager Jan. 1957 - May 1959; Millwall manger July 1959 - Jan. 1961; returning briefly to South Africa, he had posts with both the Addington and Durban City clubs before returning to manage Bedford Town late 1961 - Sep. 1963; a longer spell in South Africa later, included manager of Addington and Cape Town City. In England in Early 1970's, managed Bedford Town and Stevenage Town before retiring.

Other Honours: England (2 'full' apps.)
(Millwall) FL Div.3 (South) champions 1938

Outside-left able to take the inside-left berth also. A great favourite at The Den : a very strong forward possessing speed, two-footed rocket shooting power and ever-dangerous. Honoured as a Hitchin Town

amateur by representing both Hertfordshire and the Spartan League in his years there. JR, as the Millwall fraternity dubbed him, was of South African stock, the son of a South African rugger international. His father was a member of the Springboks' very first British touring side and the family surname was actually Schmidt.

SMITH, Leslie George Frederick
(Brentford and the Royal Air Force)
(13 England wartime apps., 3 goals)
Born: Ealing, Middlesex, 13 Mar. 1918
1938: 5-8, 11-0
Career: West London schools football; Petersham 1932; Wimbledon 1933; Hayes July 1935, also that year signing amateur forms for Brentford, turning prof. for them Mar. 1936 (he had worked in the club's office since 1933); Aston Villa Oct. 1945 (approx. £7,500); Brentford again June 1952 (£3,000); Kidderminster Harriers player/manager Aug. 1953 for a season; Wolverhampton Wanderers scout 1954-56.

Other Honours: England (1 'full' app.)
(Wimbledon) FA Amateur Cup finalist 1935

Outside-left. As will be gathererd by his appearance in a major cup final barely a month past his 17th birthday, Les Smith's was a precocious talent. This was followed by a debut for First Division Brentford in 1936/37 and, by the time war came, he was an established top flight player. Always a confident performer with the beating of most opposing defenders, he packed a hard shot. Later the proprietor of a Birmingham radio/TV business.

SOO, Frank C.

(Stoke City and the Royal Air Force)

(9 England wartime apps.)

Born: Buxton, Derbyshire, 8 Mar. 1914
Died: 25 Jan. 1991
1938: 5-7½, 11-4

Career: Liverpool schoolboy football; Prescot Cables; Stoke City Jan. 1933; Leicester City Sep. 1945 (£4,600); Luton Town as player/coach July 1946 (£3,000); Chelmsford City cs 1948; Subsequently coached in Israel and, for 5 years in Sweden. Scunthorpe United manager June 1959 - June 1960. Also managed St. Albans City for a time.

Wing-half/inside-forward. In the band of budding stars introduced by Stoke in the early 'thirties, which also included Matthews and Freddie Steele. The son of a Chinese father and an English mother, Soo shone in Merseyside schools soccer before commencing working life as a clerk. Soon discovered by Stoke City and immediately captivated the footballing public on making his first-class debut (in season 1933/34) with his polish and outstanding ball skills.

SPROSTON, Bert

(Manchester City and The Army)

(2 England wartime apps.)

Born: Elworth, nr. Sandbach, Cheshire, 22 June 1915
1938: 5-8, 12-0

Career: Sandbach Ramblers (trial with Huddersfield Town); Leeds United May 1933; Tottenham Hotspur June 1938 (£11,500); Manchester City Nov. 1938 (£11,500); retired cs 1950; Bolton Wanderers trainer July 1951, eventually scouting for that club for many years.

Other Honours: England (11 'full' apps.)
Football League (4 apps.)
(Manchester City) FL Div.2 champions 1947

Right-back certainly to be counted among the best defenders produced in the inter-war years. Sproston was coolness personified, possessed a notable tackle and was remarkably quick in recovery. Unable to settle in London he returned North in Manchester City's cause for the identical high fee Spurs paid. Actually Leeds had no wish to part with him in the first place but their financial situation at the time caused his transfer. Latterly for long associated with Bolton Wanderers.

STUBBINS, Albert

(Newcastle United)

(1 England wartime app.)

Born: Wallsend, Northumberland, 17 July 1919
1949: 5-11, 12-8

Career: Whitley & Monkseaton FC (Sunderland amateur); Newcastle United as a prof. Apr. 1937; Liverpool Sep. 1946 (£12,500); Ashington Sep. 1953; retired 1954. Subsequently scouted for Liverpool and became USA national coach in 1960.

Other Honours: Football League (4 apps.)
(Liverpool) FL champions 1947
FA Cup finalist 1950

Centre-forward. An ace goalscorer, netting for Newcastle, in all appearances an astonishing 245 in 199 outings. This included a wartime spell of 15 in 5 consecutive matches. Red-haired Albert had been brought up in the States - hence, probably, the appointment in 1960 as national coach. Afterwards he returned to this country, becoming a North-East journalist and scouting for Liverpool. During the War he was employed in a Royal Ordnance engineering works.

brother, Fred, was a goalkeeper with Oldham Athletic and other League clubs during the inter-war period. Frank was a Manchester licensee and football journalist after WW2, losing his life while persuing the latter occupation.

SWIFT, Frank Victor
(Manchester City and The Army)
(14 England wartime apps.)

Born: Blackpool, 24 Dec. 1913
Died: 6 Feb. 1958 (In the Munich air disaster)
1949: 6-2, 14-0

Career: Blackpool schools football; Blackpool Gasworks FC; Fleetwood 1931/32; Manchester City on amateur forms also in 1931/32, turning prof. Oct. 1932; retired cs 1949 but returned to make 4 FL appearances early in season 1949/50.

Other Honours: England (19 'full' apps.)
England 'B' international (1 app.)
Football League (3 apps.)
(Manchester City) FL champions 1937
FL Div.2 champions 1947
FA Cup winner 1934

Goalkeeper. A most personable player, universally popular with his natural good humour and a playing action both graceful and spectacular. His formidable physique incuded a hand span of 11½ inches. Frank had worked originally with his family's pleasure boat and, part-time, at Blackpool Gasworks. An older

SWINBURNE, Thomas Anderson
(Newcastle United and The Army)
(1 England wartime app.)

SWINBURNE
NEWCASTLE

Born: East Rainton, nr. Houghton-le-Spring, Co.
Died: Oct.-Dec. 1969
Durham, 9 Aug. 1915
1938: 5-9½, 12-4
Career: East Rainton FC; Herrington Colliery Welfare (trials with West Ham United and Hull City); Newcastle United Apr. 1934; Consett June 1947.

A sound, trustworthy performer, the 'Geordies' first choice in the two terms before war broke out and for a large part of 1946/47, the initial post-war season. Father of Trevor Swinburne, also a 'keeper, who assisted a number of FL clubs, notably Carlisle United 1977-83. Another son, Alan, made 4 League appearances guarding Oldham Athletic's goal in 1963/64. An unusual family sequence of custodians!

TAYLOR, Frank
(Wolverhampton Wanderers and The Army)
(1 England wartime app.)
Born: Barnsley, 30 Apr. 1916
Died: 10 Jan. 1970
1939: 5-8½, 10-9

Career: Barnsley Grammar School (several appearances for Barnsley FC reserves); Wolverhampton Wanderers 1933; retired through injury 1944 and invalided from Army, working for Wolves on their training staff until 1947 when he became Hull City's assistant manager to June 1948; Scarborough manager June 1948 - 1950; Leeds United 1950-52, first as coach and subsequently as assistant manager; Stoke City manager June 1952 - May 1960; was a licensee in East Yorkshire 1961-68 during which time he had a spell (from cs 1963) as a Blackburn Rovers coach.

Other Honour: (Wolves) FA Cup finalist 1939

Left-back. Played centre-forward as a schoolboy, soon reverting to full-back on joining Wolves. Succeeded his older brother, Jack, as the Molyneux club's regular left-back in 1938/39, when an ever-present, performing consistently well in a tight defence (Wolves were also Division 1 runners-up that term). Taylor's retirement in 1944 was caused by a badly damaged knee when assisting Darlington as a guest player. His later appointments at Hull and Leeds were under his old mentor, the celebrated Wolves (1927-44) manager, Major Frank Buckley.

WATSON, Willie
(Huddersfield Town and The Army)
(1 England wartime app.)
Born: Bolton-on-Dearne, Yorks., 7 Mar. 1920
1949: 5-8½, 11-4
Career: Huddersfield schools and junior football; Huddersfield Town Oct. 1937; Sunderland Apr. 1946 (£7-8,000); Halifax Town player/manager Nov. 1954 (£4,000) - Apr. 1956 when he left football until serving as Halifax Town's manager for a second spell Sep. 1964 - Apr. 1966 and Bradford City manager from Apr. 1966 - Jan. 1968.

Other Honours: England (4 'full' apps.)
England 'B' (3 apps.)

Outside-left who later made an unusual move to right-half. He was successful in both berths but probably more so in the latter, with his ball winning abilities and brainy passing. Willie was equally distinguished at cricket, with Yorkshire (1939-57) and Leicestershire

(1958-64), appearing in 23 Tests for England and serving as a Test selector 1962-64. Son of William Watson senior, Huddersfield Town's left-half in their trio of League championships, 1924-26, and FA Cup final line-ups of 1920 and 1922.

WELSH, Donald
(Charlton Athletic and The Army)
(9 England wartime apps., 12 goals)
Born: Manchester, 25 Feb. 1911
Died: 2 Feb. 1990
1938: 5-11½, 12-5½
Career: Manchester Schools; Lancashire Schools; Royal Navy football; Torquay United on amateur forms early in 1933, turning prof. July 1934; Charlton Athletic Feb. 1935 (£3,250) - Nov. 1947 when appointed Brighton & Hove Albion's secretary/manager; Liverpool manager Mar. 1951 - May 1956; Bournemouth & Bos. Ath. manager July 1958 - Feb. 1961; Wycombe Wanderers' prof. coach July 1963 - Nov. 1964. Served on Charlton Athletic's adminstrative staff for a short while from Dec. 1964.

Other Honours: England (3 'full' apps.)
Football League (1 app.)
(Charlton) FL Div.3 (South) champions 1935
FA Cup winner 1947, finalist 1946

Centre- and left-half, centre-forward and inside-left, and this super utility player could doubtless have turned in a good performance anywhere. As a forward, Don was bold, carrying a strong shot; as a defender, resilient. A multi-games player also - at cricket (Torquay CC's professional), rugby, hockey and water polo.

Outside football he had at different times been employed as a Devon licensee and youth centre manager.

WESTCOTT, Dennis
(Wolverhampton Wanderers and The Army)
(4 England wartime apps., 5 goals)
Born: Wallasey, 2 July 1917
Died: 13 July 1960
1939: 5-10, 11-11
Career: Wallasey Grocers; Leasowe Road Brickworks (Wallasey) (Everton amateur and trialist); New Brighton amateur Dec. 1935, turning prof. Jan. 1936; Wolverhampton Wanderers July 1936 (£500); Blackburn Rovers Apr. 1948; Manchester City Feb. 1950 (£12,500); Chesterfield June 1952; Stafford Rangers July 1953 for a season.

Other Honours: Football League (1 app.)
(Wolves) FA Cup finalist 1939

Centre-forward. A robust, hard running attacker, a consistent scorer throughout his first class career. He scored, for exmaple, a Football League aggregate of 172 goals in 259 outings, and, as late as Aug. 1952, netted 4 for Chesterfield against Mansfield Town. Wolves quickly moved in for Westcott after he topped New Brighton's scoring list despite making only 18 appearances, becoming an essential part of their successful late 'thirties side that climaxed as League and Cup runners-up in 1938/39

WILLIAMS, Bert Frederick

(Walsall, Wolverhampton Wanderers and the Royal
Air Force)

(4 England wartime apps.)

Born: Bilston, Staffs., 31 Jan. 1920

1950: 5-10, 12-2

Career: Bilston Schools; Thompson's FC (Wolverhampton Works
League); Walsall amateur during season 1935/36, turning prof. Apr.
1937; Wolverhampton Wanderers Sep. 1945 (£3,500); retired cs
1957.

Other Honours: England (24 'full' apps.)
England 'B' (1 app.)
Football League (5 apps.)
(Wolves) FL champions 1954
FA Cup winner 1949

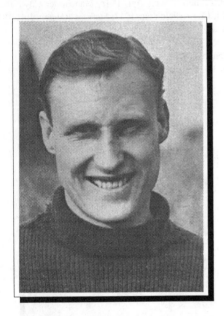

*Goalkeeper who emerged late in the War and immedi-
ate post-war period as a leading practitioner. He had
all the qualities, not least bravery and agility, and
always instilled confidence in fellow defenders.
Athletic in mien, it seems appropriate Bert should have
run a thriving sports outfitting business in his native
locality.*

WILLINGHAM, C(harles) Kenneth

(Huddersfield Town)

(6 England wartime apps.)

Born: Sheffield, 1 Dec. 1912

Died: May 1975

1938: 5-7½, 11-4

Career: Yorkshire Schools; Ecclesfield; Worksop Town; Huddersfield Town ground staff 1930, turning prof. Nov. 1931; Sunderland

Dec. 1945 (£5,000); Leeds United as player/coach Mar. 1947,
retiring from playing May 1948 and continuing as coach for a
further two years; Halifax Town coach for a spell from 1952.

Other Honours: England (12 'full' apps.)
Football League (6 apps.)
(Huddersfield) FA Cup finalist 1938

*Right-half. An exuberant performer, tireless and
especially notable for his speed. He had been a
Yorkshire schoolboy ½ mile champion in addition to
captaining the county's soccer team. At Huddersfield
linked up with established England caps, Alf Young
and Austen Campbell, to form a daunting half-back
line. Ken became a licensee on leaving the game.
Unusually he also represented England at shinty.*

WOODLEY, Victor Robert

(Chelsea)

(2 England wartime apps.)

Born: Cippenham, nr. Slough, Berks., 26 Feb. 1910

Died: 23 Oct. 1978

1938: 6-0,12-4

Career: Slough district junior football (Reading FC amateur);
Windsor & Eton (Spartan League) cs 1930; Chelsea May 1931; Bath
City Dec. 1945; Derby County Mar. 1946; Bath City again, this time
as player/manager May 1947 - Dec. 1949, when he retired.

Other Honours: England (19 'full' apps.)
Football League (4 apps.)
(Derby Co.) FA Cup winner 1946

Other Honours: England (105 'full' apps.)
England 'B' international (1 app.)
Football League (21 apps.)
(Wolves) FL champions 1954, 1958, 1959
FA Cup winner 1949

Goalkeeper. At the outbreak of hostilities very much the England No.1 with 19 consecutive appearances under his belt. Extremely competent in all aspects, his clean handling being outstanding, and completely assured. Vic made his senior debut for Chelsea soon after joining and was generally first choice thereafter despite the presence, from 1933 onwards, of Scotland's John Jackson. Latterly a licensee at Bradford-on-Avon in Wiltshire.

WRIGHT, William Ambrose
(Wolverhampton Wanderers and The Army)
(4 England wartime apps.)
Born: Ironbridge, Shropshire, 6 Feb. 1924
Died: 3 Sep. 1994
1949: 5-8, 11-7
Career: Staffordshire schoolboy football; Wolverhampton Wanderers ground staff 1938, turning prof. Feb. 1941; retired Aug. 1959; England Youth team manager/coach Oct. 1960; Arsenal manager Mar. 1962 - June 1966.

Inside-forward originally, later reverting to left-half and finally, centre-half. A world class half-back, a master in both tackling and distribution and an inspiring captain of club and country. What is more, Billy's conduct was exemplary - never sent off nor, 'tis said, ever even cautioned. Besides the honours listed above, he was 'Footballer of the Year' in 1952 and awarded the CBE in 1959. After the Arsenal appointment he worked for a television company (ATV) until retiring in 1989, finishing in a top post. Billy was also the first player to win a hundred England caps.

BARKAS, Samuel
(Manchester City)

Born: South Shields, 29 Dec. 1909

1938: 5-9, 13-7

Career: Middle Dock (Wearside League); Bradford City Aug. 1927; Manchester City Apr. 1934 (£5,000) to May 1947 when appointed Workington manager; subsequently Wigan Athletic manager and then, from 1957, a Manchester City scout and later a Leeds United scout before his last appointment running Bradford City's pools development scheme from Nov. 1964 - July 1966.

(Selected for Scotland game 2 Dec. 1939 - car crash injury en route)

Other Honours: England (5 'full' apps.)

Football League (3 apps.)

(Bradford City) FL Div.3 (North) champions 1929

(Manchester City) FL champions 1937, F.L. Div.2 champions 1947

Left back who also figured at wing-half during his Bradford City days and, on a memorable occasion, successfully deputised at inside-forward for an injured colleague in an England line-up against Belgium. Sam's versatility was but one facet in a talent that included style and constructiveness also. From a famous footballing family of four brothers prominent with League clubs during the inter-war years plus a fifth who was signed by West Bromwich Albion but did not make their first team. A cousin was Billy Felton of Sheffield Wednesday and England.

BROWN, Alan Winston
(Huddersfield Town)

Born: Corbridge, Northumberland, 26 Aug. 1914

1939: 5-11¾, 11-6

Career: Spen Black & White; Huddersfield Town Mar. 1933; Burnley Feb. 1946 (£2,000); Notts County Oct. 1948 (£12,500) retired from playing after 3 months; Sheffield Wednesday coach Jan. 1951; Burnley manager 1954 to, briefly in 1957 acting as Sheffield Wed. coach, until appointment as Sunderland manager June 1957; Sheffield Wed. manager July 1964; Sunderland manager Feb.1968 - Nov. 1972; coached in Norway and Plymouth before retiring.

(England reserve Vs. Scotland 3 Feb. 1945)

Other Honours: Football League (1 app.)

(Burnley) FA Cup finalist 1947

Centre-half. Put in a long pre-war stint understudying the England pivot, Alf Young, before coming into his own with Burnley. There he skippered the fine side that won promotion to the top flight and reached the FA Cup final in the same season) 1946-47). A real linch-pin of a centre-half; hard, uncompromising and extremely efficient. As a manager won the reputation of being a disciplinarian who could inspire, with many greatful friends aware of his warmth and humanity

---

CHISHOLM, John Richardson ("Jack")
(Tottenham Hotspur)

Born: Enfield, Middlesex, 9 Oct. 1924
Died: 24 Aug. 1977
1949: 6-2, 13-4

Career: Junior football to Tottenham Hotspur Oct. 1942 (also assisted Fulham and Millwall as a guest player during WW2); Brentford Dec. 1947 (in exchange for another player); Sheffield United Mar. 1949 (£16,000); Plymouth Argyle Dec. 1949 (£12,500) - 1954. Helston FC (Cornwall) Sep. 1955, subsequently having a spell as manager of Romford.
(England reserve Vs. Scotland 22 Apr. 1944)
Other Honour: (Plymouth Argyle) FL Div.3 (South) champions 1952

Centre-half of hefty build making a senior debut with Spurs when only 17, playing for two years until his call-up into a Guards' regiment. Considered a star of the future but sustained a serious knee injury that necessitated a long lay-off by which time other young Spurs pivots had developed and Chisholm moved on. Unlucky with injuries and during his career had cartilages removed from both knees. All the same gave Argyle, whom he skippered, excellent service in a purely defensive role. A useful cricketer for Bedfordshire and Devon, he played a single game for Middlesex. Latterly a publican.

FINNEY, Thomas
(Preston North End)

Born: Preston, Lancs. 5 Apr. 1922
1949: 5-7½, 10-6

Career: Preston Schools; Preston North End on amateur forms 1937, turning prof. Jan. 1940 (during WW2 when serving in the Tank Corps played for the British Services XI, the Wanderers, in the Middle East); retired Apr. 1960. Subsequently a Preston NE Director, club Vice-President 1973 and President, season 1975/76.

(England Vs. Switzerland 21 & 24 Jul. 1945)
Other Honours: England (76 'full' apps.)
England 'B' (1 app.)
Football League (17 apps.)
(PNE) FL Div.2 champions 1951, F.A. Cup finalist 1954

Outside-right mostly with appreciable spells at outside-left and centre-forward also. Among the finest forwards England has produced, master of a sinuous dribble that could penetrate any defence and a considerable marksmen. Twice 'Footballer of the Year' (1954 and 1957). Awarded the OBE in 1961 and the MBE in 1992. In commercial life the head of a Preston plumbing and electrical contracting firm.

HALL, Frederick W.
(Blackburn Rovers)

Born: No Place, Stanley, Co. Durham, 18 Nov. 1917
1949: 5-11, 13-12

Career: Ouston Juniors (Co. Durham); Blackburn Rovers Nov. 1935; Sunderland Aug. 1946; Barrow Sep. 1955; Ransome & Marles FC, Newark, Aug. 1956.
(England reserve Vs. France 26 May 1945)

Centre-half. As a youngster pre-war had 29 League outings for Blackburn that included appearances at right-back and wing-half also. During the War when serving in the RAF his fine 'sheet anchor' displays as a Spurs guest prompted the London club to bid for his transfer, but their offer did not meet Blackburn's valuation. Hall's move to Sunderland in 1946 came about, it was said, because of his refusal to play at full-back. Became an admired skipper of the Wearsiders. Off the field won a reputation as one of the best known pigeon fanciers in the North.

HARRIS, Frederick
(Birmingham)

Born: Sparkbrook, Birmingham, 2 July 1912
1946: 5-11½, 11-9
Career: Birmingham schoolboy football; Osborn Athletic (Birmingham); Birmingham FC Apr. 1933 (guest player for Chester during WW2); retired May 1950.
(England reserve Vs. Wales 25 Oct. 1941)
Other Honours: Football League (1 app.)
(Birmingham City) FL Div.2 champions 1948

Wing-half/inside-forward. A real Brum loyalist with over 400 first team appearances, including the war years, for the club. Captained the 1947/48 championship side from right-half, a highly competent performer in both half-back and forward positions. During the War served first with the Auxiliary Police Force and later was a corporal in the Army PTC. Qualified as a masseur, physiotherapist and chiropodist and practised at Olton, Birmingham.

HUNT, Douglas Albert
(Sheffield Wednesday)

Born: Shipton Bellinger, Hants. 19 May 1914
Died: 1989
1938: 5-11, 12-5
Career: Winchester City (Southampton amateur Jan. 1932); Tottenham Hotspur as a prof. March 1934 following a spell with their nursery club, Northfleet; Barnsley Mar. 1937; Sheffield Wednesday Mar. 1938 (£3,000); Clapton Orient Apr. 1946, becoming that club's assistant manager Aug. 1947; Gloucester City manager June 1948; subsequently Yeovil Town trainer/coach prior to a spell as Tonbridge's manager from Jan. 1954.
('England' Vs. Switzerland 21 July 1945)

Centre-forward. Succeeded the celebrated Ted Drake as Winchester City's centre and found chances at Tottenham limited by having to understudy another England cap, his namesake George Hunt, and John Morrison. Found a niche at Barnsley, however, and even more so with Wednesday, breaking that club's match scoring record (6 versus Norwich City in November 1938) and a pre-war FL aggregate 30 goals in 42 outings. During the War guested mostly for Brentford. A powerful opportunist forward.

LAYTON, William H.
(Reading)

Born: Shirley, Birmingham, 13 Jan. 1915
Died: Feb. 1984
1938: 5-10, 10-11
Career: Shirley Town; Reading Mar. 1937; Bradford (Park Avenue) Jan. 1947; Colchester United Aug. 1949 - Aug. 1950.
(England reserve Vs. Wales 5 May 1945)
Left-half/inside-left. A very useful left-sided player whose displays in both wing-half and inside-forward berths were marked by intelligence.

The war, of course, cut across his best footballing years and his peacetime League aggregate reached only 105 appearances in which he scored 22 goals. Layton did, however, gain a wartime honour by appearing in Reading's 1941 London War Cup-winning side.

Career: Junior football (Coventry City amateur); Birmingham FC amateur Sep. 1943, turning prof. the following year (guest player for Arsenal, Northampton Town and Portsmouth); Chelsea Jan. 1949 (nearly £20,000); Watford July 1952 (£7,000); retired cs 1957, subsequently player/coach for the Birmingham firm, Kynoch's, and assisted their local Works League side for some seasons from 1958. (England reserve Vs. Belgium 19 Jan. 1946)
Other Honour: (Birmingham) FL Div.2 champions 1948

Left-half. Came to England with his family as a young boy already with sporting ambitions. Developed into a class half-back of calm demeanour, the calmness underlined by successful nonchalant penalty taking. Also a master of the long distance pass. Twice a reserve for the full England team in 1946/47. Originally, it was said, more ambitious as a cricketer and, indeed, developed into a useful right-arm batsman and bowler, making 17 appearances for Warwickshire 1946-48 and also assisting Cornwall and Hertfordshire.

MITCHELL, Frank Rawlinson
(Birmingham)
Born: Goulburn, NSW, Australia, 3 June 1922
Died: 2 Apr. 1984
1949: 5-11, 12-0

STEPHENSON, J(oseph) Eric
(Leeds United)
Born: Bexleyheath, Kent, Sep. 1914
Died: Killed in action, 8 Sep. 1944

1938: 5-6½, 10-2
Career: Leeds schools and junior football; Harrogate FC; Leeds United amateur Jan. 1933, turning prof. Sep. 1934.
(England reserve Vs. Scotland 8 Feb. 1941)
Other Honours: England (2 'full' apps.)

Inside-left. Small, wily craftsman specialising in the creation of scoring opportunities for fellow forwards. Made his League debut on March 22, 1935, and after sequences of senior outings became a first choice player from the commencement of season 1937/38. Eric lost his life in the Burma campaign while serving as a major in the Gurkha Rifles.

WILLIAMS, Reginald Frederick
(Chelsea)

Born: Watford, 28 Jan. 1922
1949: 5-11, 12-8
Career: Junior football (Watford FC amateur); Chelsea amateur May 1945, turning prof. following Oct.; retired through injury Oct. 1951.
(England reserve Vs. Switzerland 11 May, & France 19 May, 1946)

Right-half/inside-right. Extremely unlucky in the way of injury, Reg's peacetime aggregate of FL and FA Cup appearances reached only 71, in which he netted 17 goals. His handy physique and generally assertive displays were, nonetheless, characterised by a graceful action.

WINTERBOTTOM, (Sir) Walter
(Manchester United)

Born: Oldham, 31 Mar. 1913
Career: Royton Amateurs (Manchester City amateur); Mossley; Manchester United amateur 1934, turning prof. May 1936; retired through injury during season 1937/38 but managed to make some guest appearances for Chelsea during WW2. Appointed as the F.A. Director of Coaching after demobilisation and was England team manager 1946-62.
(England reserve Vs. Scotland 10 Oct. 1942)

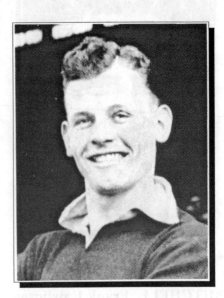

Centre-half. Once a schoolmaster, he became a highly promising pivot, good at distribution, and in positional play without being an unthinking adherent of the then fashionable 'third back' theory. His career was ended by a spinal injury. Attained fame, of course, as the long-serving and successful England manager. In wartime service with the RAF reached the rank of Wing Commander. Awarded the CBE in 1963 and knighted in 1978, the year of his appointment as an Honorary Vice-President of the FA Council.

THE CLUBS WHO SUPPLIED THE PLAYERS
and the
REFEREES

Soon after war was declared in September 1939, a number of clubs either voluntarily closed their grounds or had them 'requisitioned' for use as Air Raid Patrol Centres, Fire Stations, First Aid Posts and even Prisoner of War Camps.

This lead to some Football League clubs withdrawing completely from competitions during the war years and other having to 'ground-share'.

Arsenal played their home matches at White Hart Lane, and Manchester United shared Maine Road with Manchester City, when their main stand at Old Trafford was damaged by a bomb in 1941.

Birmingham City's St. Andrews ground was hit by bombs on a number of occasions, but they still managed to stage England's international, against Wales, on 25 October 1941 before a crowd that was limited to 25,000.

A number of other Football League club grounds were badly damaged by bombs and fire, including Plymouth Argyle, Charlton, West Ham, both the Nottingham clubs and Bramall Lane in Sheffield.

Nevertheless, a wide range of wartime League and Cup competitions were played and 36 different club provided the 90 England players involved in the 1939-46 wartime and Victory international matches.

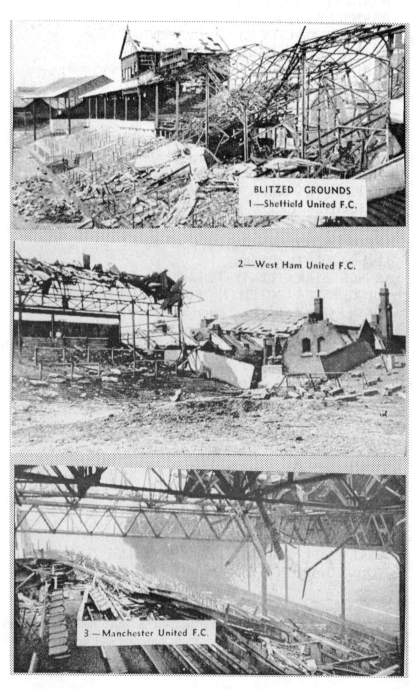

BLITZED GROUNDS
1—Sheffield United F.C.

2—West Ham United F.C.

3—Manchester United F.C.

Arsenal headed the list, providing 8 different players
with Charlton, Newcastle and Wolves, each contributing 6.

ARSENAL (8) - Compton D., Compton L., Crayston, Hapgood, B.Joy, Kirchen, Marks, Scott
ASTON VILLA (2) - Broome, Martin
BARNET (1) - L.C. Finch
BARNSLEY (1) - Harper
BIRMINGHAM CITY (2) - Harris *, Mitchell *
BLACKPOOL (2) - Mortensen, Roxburgh
BRADFORD PARK AVENUE (1) - Shackleton
BLACKBURN ROVERS (2) - Crook, Hall *
BOLTON WANDERERS (2) - Barrass, Gosling
BRENTFORD (1) - Smith L.G.F.
CHARLTON ATHLETIC (6) - Bartram, Brown R.A.J., Johnson, Oakes, Smith G.C., Welsh
CHELSEA (3) - Hanson, Williams R.F. *, Woodley
COVENTRY CITY (1) - Mason
EVERTON (4) - Britton, Greenhalgh, Lawton, Mercer
FULHAM (2) - Bacuzzi, Rooke
HUDDERSFIELD TOWN (4) - Brown A.W. *, Mountford, Watson, Willingham
LEEDS UNITED (2) - Copping, Stephenson *
LIVERPOOL (1) - Balmer
MANCHESTER CITY (4) - Barkas *, Brook, Sproston, Swift
MANCHESTER UNITED (2) - Rowley, Winterbottom *
MIDDLESBROUGH (3) - Fenton M., Hardwick, Mannion
MILLWALL (2) - Fisher F.W., Smith J.C.R.
NEWCASTLE (6) - Birkett, Clifton, Pearson, Richardson J., Stubbins, Swinburne
NOTTS COUNTY (1) - Pye
PORTSMOUTH (1) - Flewin
PRESTON NORTH END (1) - Finney *
READING (2) - M. Edelston, Layton *
SHEFFIELD UNITED (1) - Hagan
SHEFFIELD WEDNESDAY (1) - Hunt *
STOKE CITY (3) - Franklin, Matthews, Soo
SUNDERLAND (2) - Carter, Mapson
TOTTENHAM (5) - Buckingham, Chisholm *, Ditchburn, A.E. Gibbons, Hall
WALTHAMSTOW AVENUE (1) - J.W. Lewis
WEST BROMWICH ALBION (2) - Elliott, Kinsell
WEST HAM UNITED (2) - Fenton E., Goulden
WOLVERHAMPTON WANDS. (6) - Cullis, Mullen, Taylor F., Westcott, Williams B.F., Wright.

Note: Players marked with an asterisk (*), were named 'reserves' or played in the unofficial
matches in Switzerland (1945). Their biographical details appear in 'The Nearly Men' chapter.

THE REFEREES

The 36 England wartime (1939-46) and victory internationals were controlled by 28 different referees, as detailed in the tables below.

The most famous of these was, undoubtedly, the Hampshire referee, George Reader.

Reader started out as a player with St. Lukes College and joined Exeter City, as an amateur, in August 1919. He made one Southern League appearance for the Grecians against Southampton in 1919-20, scored a goal in the 4-1 win and was transferred to the Hampshire club for a £50 fee at the start of the following season.

Although he became a professional with the Saints, understudying Bill Rawlings, he continued with his studies and became a schoolmaster. His opportunities for first team football were limited to three League appearances and he was released by Southampton in May 1921.

Reader continued to combine his teaching career with playing for Cowes F.C. until he was well into his thirties, but then turned his attention to refereeing. He quickly progressed up the referees ladder, took charge of five wartime/victory internationals, the Great Britain Vs Rest of Europe match at Hampden Park in 1947 and the 1950 World Cup Finals in Brazil.

After 'putting away his whistle', Reader joined the Southampton F.C. board, became Chairman in 1963 and saw his club win the F.A. Cup in 1976, two years before passing away in July 1978 at the age of 81.

Most prominent of the Scottish wartime referees was Peter Craigmyle from Aberdeen, who refereed three of the Scotland Vs England encounters and England's victory international against Northern Ireland, in Belfast, 1945. After the war, he wrote his own biography under the title of *"A LIFETIME OF SOCCER"*. Some of his memories and observations have been included elsewhere in this book.

The Referees
for England's internationals 1939-46

Argent C.E. (Hertfordshire) Vs Wales -
Wembley 1943-44

Blackhall G.S. (Wednesbury) Vs Wales -
Birmingham 1941-42

Calder R. (Rutherglen) Vs Scotland - Hampden 1941-42 and Vs Scotland -
Hampden 1943-44

Cox J.S. (Rutherglen) Vs Scotland -
Hampden 1944-45

Craigmyle P. (Aberdeen) Vs Scotland -
Hampden 1940-41, 1942-43 and 1945-46;
Vs N. Ireland - Belfast 1945-46

Davies A.E. (Aberystwyth) Vs Wales -
Cardiff 1944-45

Delasalle M. (France) Vs Switzerland -
Chelsea 1945-46

Gow W.J. (Swansea) Vs Wales -
Cardiff 1941-42

Green Capt. F.C. (Wolverhampton) Vs
Wales - Wolverhampton 1942-43

Jewell A.J. "Jimmy" (RAF) Vs
Wales - Wembley 1939-40

Jones A. (Pontyclun) Vs Wales -
Cardiff 1940-41

McCarthy S. (Wrexham) Vs Wales -
Wrexham 1939-40

Milner F.S. (Wolverhampton) Vs Scotland -
Wembley 1941-42

Nash W.T. (Gilfach Goch) Vs Wales -
Cardiff 1944-45

Nattrass H. (Seaham) Vs Scotland -
Newcastle 1939-40

Nicholas S. (Trelewis) Vs Wales -
Cardiff 1939-40

Reader G. (Hampshire) Vs Wales - Wembley
1942-43 - West Bromwich 1945-46; Vs
Scotland - Wembley 1944-45; Vs France -
Wembley 1944-45; Vs Belgium - Wembley
1945-46.

Ross-Gower Sgt. W.E. (Scots Guards) Vs
Scotland - Wembley 1941-42

Scherz M. (Switzerland) Vs France -
Paris 1945-46

Smith T. (Atherstone) Vs Scotland -
Villa Park 1944-45

Snape P. (Manchester) Vs Scotland -
Maine Road 1943-44

Stevens P. (Bedfordshire) Vs Scotland -
Wembley 1942-43

Tedds G. (Nottingham) Vs Wales -
Nottingham 1940-41

Thompson T. (Leamington) Vs Scotland -
Newcastle 1940-41

Warren T.J. (Llwynpis) Vs Wales -
Cardiff 1942-43

Webb W. (Glasgow) Vs Scotland -
Hampden 1939-40

Wood W.E. (Bedfordshire) Vs Scotland -
Wembley 1943-44

Wort F.W. (Kent) Vs Wales -
Anfield 1944-45

During the initial research into the Victory internationals of 1945-46, it was noted that two matches were played against Switzerland in July 1945.

However, whilst the line-ups were included in THE HISTORY OF THE FOOTBALL ASSOCIATION (published in 1953), they were annotated 'These two teams were Combined services XI's, not full internationals'.

During the war, several Combined Services, Army and RAF representative matches were played but couldn't be regarded as 'internationals' and initially, it was thought that these two 1945 matches, against Switzerland, fell into this category. Further research in Tommy Lawton's book, FOOTBALL IS MY BUSINESS (Sporting Handbooks, 1946) revealed that he regarded

Andreoli (Switzerland) comes across to tackle Lawton (21 July)

them as England 'internationals' and both Harry Kinsell and Willie Watson confirmed that the match against Switzerland in which they played, is recorded along with their other England Victory international appearances on the illuminated address awarded to all England wartime internationalists, by The Football Association, in April 1946.

The menu card from the after match Dinner, given by the Swiss F.A. in Berne on 21 July 1945, clearly indicates that this was for the 'Schweiz/ England' match and an action photo from the game shows Lawton wearing the England badge on his shirt.

The war with Germany was over in May 1945 and the Football Association of Switzerland (who were a 'neutral' country

The England team line-up for the match on the 21st July.

during the war) invited The Football Association to send a party over to play two matches in Berne and Zurich on 21 and 24 July 1945, respectively.

The players chosen - all Englishmen and most of them 'full' or wartime internationals already - gathered in London only to find that the Air Ministry had cancelled the plane in which they were to fly, and had in fact refused permission for air transport for the party.

It was too late to make arrangements for the party to travel to Switzerland by boat and train, but at the last minute the Swiss Government offered to arrange the air transport.

On the morning of 18 July 1945 a message was received at Croydon that a Swiss passenger plane - the first to leave that country for England since September 1939 - wished to land.

After some delay the Air Ministry gave it permission to land and the players and officials were flown to Duebendorf Airport, Zurich.

On arrival, the party was transported to Berne by train and after a couple of days training and sightseeing the first of the two 'England' Vs Switzerland matches was played on 21 July 1945, in Berne.

The 'England' line-up was; Swift(Manchester City), Scott(Arsenal), Hardwick (Middlesbrough), Soo(Stoke), Franklin(Stoke), Mercer(Everton, Capt.), Finney(Preston), Brown R.A.J.(Charlton), Lawton(Everton), Hunt(Sheffield Wednesday) and Smith L.G.F.(Brentford).

The Swiss team had been away for three weeks special training in the woods and were far too fit for a rather jaded bunch of British servicemen who had come straight from Army camps or Air Force stations for this trip. Tom Finney, then a relatively unknown uncapped winger with Preston North End, had only arrived a couple of days before this trip from Austria, where he was stationed with the Central Mediterranean Forces.

The small ground was packed to capacity with around 35,000 spectators, many of whom were sitting on the edge of the pitch only a few inches from the touchlines!

Despite a magnificent display by Frank Swift, goals by Fink, Friedlander and Amado gave the Swiss team a comfortable 3-1 win. 'Sailor' Brown (Charlton) scored England's goal.

At the final whistle the excited crowd swarmed across the ground to carry Swift shoulder high from the pitch.

The next day, the England party left for Neufeld to watch an athletics meeting which included the, then, world's fastest milers - Gundar Haegg and Arne Andersson - in action. Andersson fairly flew around the track to beat the Swiss 1,500 metres record by three seconds!

After further sightseeing trips in the Bernese Oberland, the party moved on to Zurich, to play their second match on 24 July 1945.

England fielded; Swift, Scott, Kinsell(Bolton); Mercer(capt.), Franklin, Fenton E.; (West Ham), Finney, Fenton M.

(Middlesbrough), Lawton, Smith L.G.F. and Watson(Huddersfield Town), against a Swiss "B" team who a few days earlier had beaten the full national team (who had beaten England in Berne) 3-1 in a trial match!

However, this time the England team having rested and enjoyed some magnificent meals, after six years of food rationing back at home, were more than a match for their Swiss hosts.

Tom Finney opened the scoring, with a header from a Willie Watson cross, after just four minutes. Eighteen minutes later, Watson himself scored a picture goal cracking the ball home from a long way out. Mickey Fenton scored with a superb first-time drive to give England a comfortable 3-0 win.

These two matches enabled Finney to show the England officials what he could do and, after the war, he went on to win 76 full caps for his country.

Although not included in the full detailed lists of England line-ups and goalscorers, elsewhere in this book, the fact that only English players were included in the party and The Football Association included both matches in their end of the war Illuminated Address's awarded to all the 1939-46 England players, they should be recognised alongside all the other wartime and victory internationals.

THE 'DOUBLE' INTERNATIONALS

Before the football and cricket seasons overlapped, it wasn't unusual for professional footballers to also appear in county cricket matches during the summer months.

Several England international footballers, including wartime 'caps' Raich Carter, Denis and Leslie Compton, Ted Drake, E.H. 'Patsy' Hendren and Willie Watson, also played county cricket and three of these even won international honours at both sports.

Denis Compton (left) and Patsy Hendren, coming out to bat for Middlesex against Surrey in 1936. Compton was 18 at the time, and Hendren was 47 years old.

1920/21. During the next fourteen years he played in 51 Tests for England.

His greatest personal triumph was the visit to the West Indies in 1929/30, when he hit no less than four double centuries during the tour, and a total of 1,765 runs at an average of 137.76 - a record which still stands. Hendren's highest Test score was 205 not out against the West Indies, at Port of Spain in 1929/30, and his highest first-class innings was 301 not out for Middlesex against Worcestershire, at Dudley in 1933.

Back in 1907, at the age of 18, **'Patsy' Hendren** started a cricket career with Middlesex that was to last 30 years, during which time he played 581 games for his county.

Hendren was a middle order right-hand batsman, right-arm slow bowler, and an excellent deep fielder.

Having been 'capped' for England at soccer in the 1919 Victory international against Wales, 'Patsy' earned his 'double international' tag when he was selected for his first Test cricket appearance in the MCC's tour of Australia during the winter of

In all he hit 22 first-class innings of 200 or more and at the end of his Test career in 1935 he had averaged 47.63 runs for England in 83 innings, spread over 51 Test matches. Towards the end of his first-class cricket career with Middlesex, Hendren was joined by another promising young batsman who went on to become one of England's most accomplished and famous cricketers - and a 'double' international, too!

During the height of his cricket career, **Denis Compton's** face was a familiar sight on advertising hoardings and in newspaper and magazine advertisements. From these he was affectionately known as the 'Brylcream Boy' due to his immaculate grooming and endorsement of the most popular haircream of the day.

Compton joined Middlesex as an 18 year-old, in 1936, and during the next 22 years he appeared in 296 matches for the county. Like Hendren, he was a right-hand middle order batsman and also developed into a more than useful slow left-arm bowler.

Although he made his Test debut for England in 1937, his football commitments with Arsenal prevented him touring overseas with the MCC until 1946/47, although he made many runs for the wartime 'England' team whilst with the Army in India.

Compton became a 'double' international when he made his first soccer appearance for England at outside-left against Wales at Wembley on 13 April 1940. Despite missing all of the pre-war MCC tours, Compton still clocked-up 78 Test appearances for England and in 131 innings amassed 5,807 runs, at an average of 50.06, and also took 25 Test wickets - his best bowling figures for England being 5 wickets for 70 runs.

Of all his many achievements in a 22 year career with Middlesex, Compton's greatest year was in 1947. He created new records both for the most runs in first-class cricket in a season, and most centuries, when he scored 3,816 runs at an average of 90.85, and 18 centuries.

The South African tourists conceded 6 centuries to Compton in the summer of 1947 and he amassed 753 runs, at an average of 94.12, in the Test matches against them.

In the tour to South Africa in the winter of 1948/49, Compton recorded his highest score of 300 for the MCC against North-East Transvaal, in just 181 minutes - the fastest triple hundred ever made in a first-class match!

Compton won an F.A. Cup winners medal with Arsenal in 1950, but several operations on an old soccer injury restricted his movement and his cricket Test career ended after the 1956/57 tour to South Africa.

By the time his first-class cricket career had come to an end in 1958, he had accumulated a total of 38,942 runs (Av. 51.85) and had taken a total of 622 wickets at a cost of 32.27 runs each.

Although both Hendren and Compton can, quite rightly, claim to be 'double' internationals, their soccer appearances for England were restricted to the 'unofficial' wartime matches.

The only wartime England international player who went on to be capped at 'full' international level and also played in Test matches for his country was **Willie Watson**, who played soccer for Huddersfield Town, Sunderland and Halifax Town and cricket for both Yorkshire and Leicestershire.

Watson started his football career with Huddersfield Town in 1937 and joined Yorkshire County Cricket Club in 1939. The War interrupted his cricket career, but on 20 October 1945 Watson earned his first soccer international honour when he was chosen to play for England, at outside-left, against Wales at West Bromwich. After the war Watson resumed his cricket with Yorkshire, but it was his move to Sunderland F.C. in 1946 that really lead to his football career taking-off.

He made three appearances for the England 'B' team and four full international appearances between 1949 and 1950. The England cricket selectors were also taking notice of the stylish middle order left-hand batsman, and he was put in something of a dilemma when the football selectors asked him if he would be available for the squad for the 1950 World Cup in Brazil.

When Watson was over in this country last summer, for the Test matches against South Africa - which has been his home for the past 25 years, he told the Author: *"By this time I was a regular in the Yorkshire County Cricket team and a possible for an England cricket cap. After much heart-searching I told The Football Association that I would have to confine my football to the winter and cricket in the summer.*

"But when they asked me to reconsider, I consulted the Yorkshire Committee and they gave me their blessing to join the England squad in Brazil. I didn't play in any of England's three matches, but it was an unforgettable experience".

After this football tour he concentrated on his cricket and the following year he made his first appearance for England in a Test Match against South Africa. Between 1951 and the MCC winter tour to Australia and New Zealand in the winter of 1958/59, Watson played in 23 Test matches for England. He scored 879 runs in 37 innings (Av. 25.85), including one innings of 116, but his highest first-class innings was 257 for the MCC against British Guiana at Georgetown during the tour of the West Indies in 1953/54.

During 18 years with Yorkshire he played 283 matches, but in 1958 he moved on to Leicestershire and captained the county until 1961.

In 1962 he was appointed a Test selector, finally retiring from the first-class game in 1964. In a cricket career spanning 25 years, Watson played in 468 matches and scored 25,670 at a very commendable average of 39.86 runs an innings.

Apart from Arthur Milton (Arsenal, Bristol City and Gloucestershire), who won one England soccer cap against Austria in 1951 and six Test appearances for the England cricket team between 1958 and 1959, there hasn't been another 'double' international since.

With the football and cricket seasons now both being spread over almost the whole of the year, it is unlikely we shall ever see another sportsmen who wins international honours for his country at football and cricket.

Willie Watson · Huddersfield, Sunderland, Yorkshire and Leicestershire, plus 'double' England.

DID YOU KNOW THAT........

A MISCELLANY OF FACTS ON WARTIME INTERNATIONAL FOOTBALL

The Football National War Fund, for the assistance of players killed or injured while engaged on service or other work directly involved with the Great War, and their immediate relatives, was founded on 12 December 1917, at a Conference held in Derby, by The Football Association. The F.A. took the first practical step by handing over, to the new body, the capital of their Benevolent Fund - £5,000. In May 1918 The Football League gave £1,000 and receipts from matches brought the total up to £10,000, that month. The Fund was under the control of the leading authorities and was applicable to ALL footballers.

****

Match receipts for the first 1919 Victory International against Scotland, at Goodison Park, totalled £3,369 but, although there were more than twice as many spectators at the return match at Hampden Park, receipts there only amounted to £3,650.

****

The Victory international match between England and Wales at Stoke City's Victoria Ground, was originally scheduled to be played on Saturday 4 October 1919, but was postponed due to a Railway Strike. The match was eventually played two weeks later, on 18 October 1919. Were **two** different programmes issued for the match? Not even one has been tracked down!

****

England's team for the first wartime international, against Wales at Ninian Park on 11 November 1939, was picked entirely from London clubs - and six of the Welsh team were from clubs in the capital too! Arsenal provided five players for the match - three for England and two for Wales.

****

Jim Lewis, the Walthamstow Avenue amateur, became England's first-ever 'substitute', when he came on for the injured Joe Bacuzzi (Fulham), in the match at Cardiff in 1939.

Lewis, who had played League football for Queens Park Rangers before the war, was 34 years old, by then, and this was his only wartime international appearance for England.

Large parties of wounded soldiers from Africa - many of them the guest of Lord Davies (President of the Welsh F.A.) - watched this Wales Vs England game from special vantage points in the Ninian Park ground.

****

Included in the crowd of 17,000 at Wrexham, for the Wales Vs England game, were 300 soldiers who had route marched 12 miles, from their Army camp to be there!

****

Sam Barkas and Eric Brook, both from Manchester City, were injured in a three-car pile-up, at Wath-on-Dearne, Yorkshire, on their way to play for England against Scotland at Newcastle on 2 December 1939. The pair were replaced by two Newcastle players - Joe Richardson and Tom Pearson. The latter was, in fact, a Scot who was subsequently capped for Scotland against England and Belgium in 1947 and for the Scottish League against The Football League, whilst with Aberdeen.

****

In England's first wartime match at Wembley - Vs Wales 13 April 1940 - a long range shot from Arsenal's Bryn Jones slipped through Sam Bartram's hands, Willie Hall (England) missed a penalty, and Wales won 1-0!

****

It was rumoured that the Scotland Vs England match at Hampden Park, on 11 May 1940, would not be played. A German radio propaganda broadcast forecast that the Luftwaffe would make a raid on the game during the second half.

This caused 6,000 fans to stay away, but 75,000 fans defied the enemy and saw the two teams draw 1-1.

Sam Bartram (Charlton) was due to play in this match, at Hampden Park, but the RAF refused him leave to travel up to Glasgow and Vic Woodley (Chelsea) was drafted into the England goal.

****

The first match of the 1940-1 season was played on 8 February 1941. Scotland beat England 3-2, at St. James' Park, Newcastle, Joe Bacuzzi (Fulham) having the misfortune to score the winning 'own' goal, with a misplaced back-header.

****

The first wartime international hat-trick was scored by Don Welsh (Charlton) at the City Ground Nottingham on 26 April 1941. In fact, Welsh scored all four goals for England in their 4-1 win over Wales.

****

Johnny Mapson was selected to play in goal for England against Wales at Cardiff on 7 June 1941, but withdrew to play for Reading in the London War Cup Final.

This Final was scheduled to be played on the same day, at Chelsea's Stamford Bridge Ground. Reading won the Final 3-2, but, unfortunately, Mapson was never selected to play for England again!

****

Prime Minster Winston Churchill was guest of honour at the England Vs Scotland match at Wembley on 4 October 1941 and was introduced to players of both sides prior to the match.

****

Despite being severely bomb-damaged, the England Vs Wales international of 25 October 1941 was played at Birmingham City's St. Andrews ground.

Winston Churchill meets Denis Compton.

The crowd was restricted to 25,000 and the match - the first international at this ground - was a complete sell-out!

Mrs. Churchill is introduced to Ken Willingham

The England Vs Scotland game at Wembley, on 17 January 1942, was played in thick snow and the pitch markings were painted in blue to stand-out against the white surroundings.

Tommy Walker the former Hearts and Scottish international, loaned his own personal collection of jerseys to the Scottish team, who were short of kit due to clothing coupons being in short supply.

The match was in aid of Mrs Churchill's 'Aid to Russia' Fund and the Prime minister's wife was presented to both teams, prior to the match.

****

Scotland beat England 5-4, before the biggest attendance of the 1941-42 season, in the match at Hampden Park on 18 April 1942. Jimmy Hagan (Sheffield United) scored after just 50 seconds and both centre-forwards - Lawton (England) and Dodds (Scotland) - scored hat-tricks. Bill Shankley (then with Preston North End) scored the winner in the most competitive game of the war period that was played between the old rivals.

****

England goalkeeper George Marks (Arsenal) was injured after 20 minutes of the match against Wales of Cardiff on 9 May 1942, but played on - no goalkeeper substitutes in those days! After the match Marks was taken to hospital where it was discovered he had sustained quite severe internal injuries.

****

Arthur 'Jack' Smith, a full-back with Wolves was selected by England for one of the 1941-42 internationals, but was 'dropped' 48 hours before the game when it was discovered that he was born in Aberaman and had represented Wales at Schoolboy level 15 years earlier! Smith was subsequently 'capped' **for** Wales in a wartime international.

****

England's 0-0 draw with Scotland, at Wembley on 4 October 1942, was only the second goalless match in the history of the encounters between the two countries. The previous scoreless draw was in the inaugural game 70 years earlier! King George of the Hellenes and King Kaakon of Norway both attended the match, as guests of The Football Association.

****

The gate receipts of £12,500, from the attendance of 75,000 from the England Vs Wales match at Wembley on 27 February 1943, was donated to the Prisoner of War and Aid to Russia Funds.

'Man in the Middle' for this match was former Southampton centre-forward George Reader - the first ex-professional footballer to referee an England international match.

The players were presented to King George VI before the start of the match.

Raich Carter scores England's third goal in the 5-3 victory.

England centre-half Stan Cullis (Wolves) was injured in an off the ball incident in the match against Scotland at Hampden on 17 April 1943.

England won 4-0 and after the match a Scotland F.A. official stated that the offending player would never play for Scotland again!

****

September 25 1943, was another historic 'first' in the record of substitutions. Welsh left-half Ivor Powell (Q.P.R.) was injured in the match against England at Wembley. The score, at the time, was 4-1 to the home team, and England reserve, Stan Mortensen (Blackpool) was allowed to come-on for Wales, for the remainder of the game! Mortensen took-up the inside-left position, with Ron Burgess (Spurs) reverting to left-half.

Wales pulled back to 4-3, but England scored another four goals to give them a convincing 8-3 victory. Mortensen **wasn't** one of the Welsh goalscorers!

****

England rattled-in another eight goals, against Scotland at Maine Road, Manchester, on 16 October 1943, and followed this with another six against Scotland (again), at Wembley, on 19 February 1944.

Princess Elizabeth (now the Queen) attended the latter game, her first ever football match, and was accompanied in the stand by Field Marshall Montgomery.

****

The match between Scotland and England at Hampden on 22 April 1944 attracted a, then, record wartime crowd of 133,000, with receipts of £23,000. The price of stand seats for the match was raised to 30 shillings each (£1.50) - quite a high price in those days.

****

England completed their 100% record for the 1943-44 season with a 2-0 win over Wales at Ninian Park on 6 May 1944.

****

Reg Flewin (Portsmouth) became the first serviceman from the Royal Navy to be picked for England during the war, when he lined-up at centre-half in the match against Wales at Anfield on 16 September 1944.

****

Amateur international Bernard Joy (Arsenal) took-over the number '5' shirt for the match against Scotland at Wembley on 14 October 1944, which England won 6-2.

****

At bomb-scarred Villa Park, the stand seats had to be recovered from the Birmingham air-raid shelters - where they had been stored in case the ground received a direct hit from one of Hitler's bombers - in time for the England Vs Scotland on 3 February 1945. 66,000 saw England beat the Scots 3-2.

****

Scotland wore numbered shirts, for the first time, in the match against England at Hampden on 14 April 1945 and a minute's silence was observed, due to the death of American President Roosevelt the previous day.

The Scots suffered their seventh successive defeat against England and their worst-ever beating at Hampden - 1-6 - as well as losing their number '8', Bogan, after 40 seconds following a collision with England goalkeeper Swift.

Bogan's appearance for just 40 seconds - he was never selected for Scotland again - and was certainly the shortest wartime international career, if not of ALL TIME!

****

Raich Carter scored all three goals in England's 3-2 win over Wales at Ninian Park, Cardiff on 5 May 1945. Hostilities with Germany ended, and V.E. Day was declared, four days later.

****

England played their first match against foreign opposition for six years, when France were invited to Wembley in the first of the Victory internationals, on 26 May 1945.

****

On 15 September 1945, England made their first trip across the Irish Sea for almost seven years, to play Northern Ireland in Belfast.

A single goal, from Stan Mortensen, gave England a 1-0 victory in front of an enthusiastic crowd of 45,061, who had been starved of international football for more than six years.

****

Despite some press reports to the contrary, Harry Kinsell (West Bromwich) and George Lowrie (Coventry City) - representing England and Wales, respectively - were **NOT** sent off in the Victory international match played at The Hawthorns, 20 October 1945 (see Harry Kinsell's 'Personal Reminiscences' elsewhere in this book).

****

Billy Wright, who after the war went on to become the first England player to win 100 caps, made his first appearance for England in the Victory international against Belgium at Wembley on 19 January 1946.

Jesse Pye (Notts County), who later joined Wright at Wolves, scored on his international debut, and another goal from Charlton's 'Sailor' Brown gave England a 2-0 win.

****

Scotland set a wartime international attendance record, when 139,468 packed into Hampden Park to see the Scots defeat England 1-0.

****

The 'amateurs' from Switzerland met England's 'professionals' for the first time in an international at Stamford Bridge on 11 May 1946.

****

The final Victory international of 1945-46 was played against France, in Paris, on 19 May 1946.

England lost 2-1, and in so doing, Raich Carter - playing in his 17th wartime international - lost his record of never being in a losing England international team.

In the same match, Joe Bacuzzi (Fulham) set a unique record of being the only Englishman to have played in the 'first' (Vs Wales at Cardiff on 11 November 1939) and 'last' wartime internationals.

****

Although Frank Swift served in the Army during World War Two, he started off as a wartime policeman. On his first day on traffic point duty, in Manchester, he became so confused he left his post and let the traffic sort itself out!

****

University graduate Bernard Joy remained an amateur playing with Arsenal and England. After his career as a school teacher, he became a football journalist with both *The Star* and *Evening Standard*, and could often be seen in the Wembley Press Box when he was well into his sixties.

****

The Team Attendant (equivalent to today's Coach or Assistant Manager) for several of England's World War Two internationals was Millwall Trainer, Bill Voisey - who played for England in the 1919 Victory international at Cardiff

****

Marks, the wartime Arsenal goalkeeper, has always been referred to as 'George' and every previous reference book has always listed him as 'Marks G.W.', whereas he was actually christened 'William George Marks', a fact discovered from a visit made by the Author.

Bill Voisey

****

The oldest living England wartime internationalist must be Lester Finch (Barnet) who was born on 26 August 1909. It is doubtful if there is an older living Scottish or Welsh wartime international either - unless somebody knows better!

****

A selection of personal reminiscences and anecdotes from some of the England players, a 'ballboy' and a referee who were involved in the wartime internationals.

RANDOM REMINISCENCES

BRYAN HAWKINS (1940's Wembley Ball Boy)

"I lived in Wembley (the area, not the Stadium!), from 1932 until 1958 and I believe I saw every wartime international played there, including Belgium Vs Holland in 1941.

"During the war, the ballboys for the matches played at Wembley Stadium were Boy Scouts picked from various Wembley troops, and I was lucky enough to be selected four times including one match between the RAF and Police.

"At the internationals, the ballboys waited in the tunnel, with the players, and then ran out just in front of the teams. We had strict instructions NOT to kick the ball back, but to always throw it or hand it to the players.

"During one match I attempted to retrieve the ball and throw it back to Frank Soo (Stoke City). Unfortunately, the ball struck part of the fence and bounced back onto the greyhound track. By this time Soo was snapping his fingers and shouting "Hurry up, son"! I jumped over the fence, grabbed the ball, and threw it with great haste. This time it struck the linesman on the back of the head and rolled down the pitch. Soo decided to fetch it himself and Joe Mercer (England's captain) thought it was a great joke, as did most of the crowd. Was my face red!

"I was a keen collector of sporting autographs and used to try and get the signatures on cigarette cards. Being a ballboy at Wembley, gave me direct access to the players just before and after the match. I had a card of Joe Mercer, from the Wills Association Footballers series, and he autographed it for me after the above match, but I didn't have the nerve to ask Frank Soo. So my Churchmans No.41 card, from the Association Footballers series, remained unsigned!"

CHURCHMAN'S CIGARETTES

F. SOO (STOKE CITY,

Author's note - Bryan Hawkins was called up to do his National Service in 1946 and missed some of the Victory internationals at Wembley. However, he became a very useful athlete, whilst he was in the RAF, and represented Great Britain in the 1954 European Championships in Berne and came 5th in the 10,000m walk.

....

W.H. (BERT) JOHNSON (Charlton Athletic)

"My two appearances for England were in the Victory internationals against Switzerland at Stamford Bridge, and France in Paris in 1946, soon after I played for Charlton in the F.A. Cup Final.

"I remember the French goalkeeper, Da Rui, was carried shoulder high, after the Paris match, and he was given a '10 out of 10' rating in the French magazine L'Equipe. Goalkeepers can only stop saveable shots, and it was our finishing that was at fault, which made his day. It we had got a second goal I'm sure we would have gone on to win comfortably, but that's football!"

WALTER WINTERBOTTOM (Manchester United)

"Although I played for an F.A. XI against an RAF XI, at Luton on 6 June 1942, my only international selection was as a reserve for England against Scotland, at Wembley on 10 October 1942."

....

J.C.R. (REG) SMITH (Millwall)

"When I used to play as an amateur for Hitchin Town, I remember playing against Barnet many times. Their outside-left was Lester Finch and we were rivals for the left-winger's place in the Hertfordshire county team for many years.

"I turned professional for Millwall in August 1935. Lester remained an amateur and went on to win many amateur caps for England. But we were both capped for England in wartime internationals later in our careers."

....

REG WILLIAMS (Chelsea)

"My selection as 'reserve' for the England team, against Switzerland at Stamford Bridge in 1946, was a pleasant surprise.

"When I received a further letter from Stanley Rous, Secretary of the Football Association, telling me of my selection for the England match in Paris, it was a bitter pill to swallow when I didn't actually get a game. I finished-up non-playing reserve, again!"

....

THE FOOTBALL ASSOCIATION.

PATRON :
HIS MAJESTY THE KING.
PRESIDENT :
THE RT. HON. THE EARL OF ATHLONE, K.G.

SECRETARY :
S. F. ROUS, C.B.E.

TELEGRAPHIC ADDRESS :
"FOOTBALL ASSOCIATION
PADD. LONDON."

22, LANCASTER GATE,
LONDON · W. 2.

May 1946

Dear Sir,

International Match
FRANCE v. ENGLAND

I am pleased to inform you that you have been selected to play for England in the above match to be played in Paris on May 19.

In the case of Service players, an application for leave of absence has been made to Commanding Officers.

Enclosed is a French Visa Form for completion and return to this office immediately.

A programme of Arrangements and Instructions will be sent within the course of a few days.

Please complete the attached slip and return it to me with the Visa Form.

Yours sincerely,

S. Rous.
Secretary

JOHNNY MAPSON
(Sunderland)

"I can't remember much about my appearance for England against Wales, at Nottingham Forest on 26 April 1941, but I know we won comfortably 4-1, and Don Welsh scored all our goals.

"The return match against Wales, that season, was due to be played at Cardiff on 7 June 1941.

I was picked to play again, but the match clashed with the London War Cup Final. I was working for an Engineering Company in Reading at the time, and although I was still on Sunderland's books I was allowed to guest for Reading, which was, of course, the club that gave me my first chance in professional football.

"The manager asked me if I would play in this important London War Cup Final at Stamford Bridge, and I withdrew from the England team - Sam Bartram (Charlton) taking my place. Reading won the London War Cup, beating Brentford 3-2, and I didn't regret my decision. However, I was never picked for England again, and I have always wondered if my withdrawal from the match against Wales, and the fact that I wasn't a 'serviceman' - I was in a 'reserved' occupation and was never called-up despite volunteering for service in the Army or RAF - had anything to do with it!"

....

LESTER FINCH (Barnet)

"Although I had already played many times for the England amateurs, the 1936 Great Britain Olympic team, and had toured Australia, New Zealand and South Africa with Football Association representative teams, I was thrilled to be selected for an F.A. XI against The Army, at Newcastle, in May 1941.

"I scored a couple of goals, in our 4-1 win, and thought it must have been this performance that led to me being picked for the full England team, to play Wales at Ninian Park, Cardiff on 7 June 1941. It was a memorable occasion for me, an amateur, to play alongside such great players as Eddie Hapgood, Stan Cullis, George Male, Jimmy Hagan and Cliff Britton. We won 3-2 and it was a wonderful way to end the season for me."

....

GEORGE MARKS (Arsenal)

"I had already played in a Wembley Cup Final for Arsenal when I was selected for my first international, against Scotland in October 1941, but it was a great honour to play for my country.

"I played in all five of the England matches of 1941-42 and the first three of 1942-43. One of my team-mates, in three of the matches was Maurice Edelston of Reading, who was still an amateur in those days. He had turned professional by the time I joined him at Elm Park in 1948, but Maurice was still teaching at the Sonning Bluecoat School, whilst playing for Reading's first team."

BERT SPROSTON (Manchester City)

"Whilst I was travelling up to Glasgow, from Crewe, on the Friday before the match against Scotland (11 May 1940), the hostilities really got started. As we stopped at various stations on our journey, news came through that Germany had started their bombing and that Austria was on fire. Lord Haw Haw, in one of his German radio propaganda broadcasts, said he hoped the people of Scotland enjoyed half the match as the Germans would bomb Hampden Park at half-time!

"We could see British fighter planes circling the stadium throughout the match, just in case the Germans tried to carry out their threat, but 75,000 fans still packed into Hampden Park to see us hold the Scots to a 1-1 draw.

"When I went on a refresher course at Aldershot I was told to report to the regional Training Officer at Glasgow and spent the next 8½ months on the Troopship Strathard, helping the remedials.

"My Army commitments didn't give me many opportunities to play much football during the remainder of the war and I never played for England again."

....

JOE BACUZZI (Fulham)

"When I was called-up I went into the REME and after training at Aldershot, I was posted to Arborfield, near Reading. I guested for Reading, at Elm Park, but was still able to play for Fulham, quite regularly.

"One of my biggest thrills was being introduced to King George VI, when I was playing for England against Scotland in a wartime international at Wembley.

"At the end of the war we played a Victory international against France in Paris. The food was wonderful, but I was used to good cooking as my father was a chef at London's Trocadero Restaurant."

....

STAN CULLIS (Wolves)

"Although I played in 20 of England's wartime internationals, I might have played in more, if I hadn't been posted to Italy. Neil Franklin took my place. My greatest memories were the amazing crowds who turned-up for the matches against Scotland, especially those at Hampden Park. We beat Scotland 4-0 at Hampden in April 1943 and when we were due to play them again, at Maine Road Manchester the following October, the Scottish newspapers tipped their team to win, due to the influx of new players into their side. As it turned out, Tommy Lawton scored 4 goals and we won 8-0!

"Stanley Matthews was an automatic choice for England throughout the war years, and I think he enjoyed these internationals more than any other time during his career."

HARRY CLIFTON (Newcastle)

"I can recall scoring one of the goals in my only wartime international against Scotland, at Newcastle, in 1939. But when I got called-up in 1941 I toured with the British Wanderers in Turkey."

....

WILLIE WATSON (Huddersfield Town)

"I was only 19 years old, when war broke out, and had played less than a dozen first team games for Huddersfield when League Football was suspended in September 1939. I played in every forward position during their first season in a Regional War League, and when I was called up I played in a number of representative matches for The Army.

"My first international recognition was when I was selected for the England squad to play in Switzerland, in July 1945. I played in the match in Zurich, layed-on a goal for Tom Finney, and managed to score one myself in our 3-0 win.

"When the 1945-46 season got under way, I was selected to play for England in the Victory international, against Wales, at West Bromwich Albion's ground. At the time I was regarded as an outside-left, and was selected for England in that position. However, I had always preferred playing at wing-half, and it was for this reason that I left Huddersfield Town, after the war, to join Sunderland.

"I think I did the right thing, for I soon established myself as a wing-half and won my full England caps, in that position, in the late 1940's."

....

LEN SHACKLETON (BPA/Newcastle/Sunderland)

"My one England appearance during the war was the Victory international against Scotland in 1946.

"There were almost 140,000 spectators at Hampden Park. I recall the Football Association only allowed me a 3rd Class railway ticket to travel to Glasgow, and my match fee was thirty shillings (£1.50)! My wife went to the game and paid her own expenses - rail fare and hotel accommodation.

"During the war I worked for G.E.C. as a fitter. Despite volunteering for the RAF, Fleet Air Arm, Navy and Army, I wasn't allowed to be released from my job. When the war was over I was 'made' into a 'Bevin Boy' - down the coalmine!"

....

ALBERT STUBBINS (Liverpool)

"My only appearance for England was against Wales, at West Bromwich in 1945. My clearest recollection from the game was a save from the Welsh keeper, Cyril Sidlow. During the first half I drove a ball hard and low to Cyril's left hand, aiming just inside the post, but somehow he got his fingers to the ball and pushed it round the post for a corner kick. Cyril and I were both team mates at Liverpool."

HARRY KINSELL (West Bromwich)

"As well as playing in the two Victory internationals against Ireland and Wales in 1945, I was also in the 'England' (sic) team that played in Switzerland in June 1945. As most of the team were still in the armed forces, we had to go home and change into civvies before we went to Switzerland. You can imagine what a motley crew we looked, in clothes that were pre-war and not the best of fits. We couldn't wear our uniforms as we were visiting a neutral country and we were still at war with Japan. We flew out by a Swiss airline and it was the first plane to arrive in England from Switzerland, since the outbreak of the war. It was a glorious two weeks and we played two matches. My outstanding memory was the endless food provided at mealtimes, after we had suffered rationing for so long. I was also able to kit myself out with 'new togs'. My family hardly recognised me when I returned home!

"During the match against Wales, at West Bromwich in 1945, there was an incident when George Lowrie and I were involved in a bit of a scuffle. We were both reprimanded by the referee, but neither of us was sent off - despite some newspaper reports to the contrary! George and I were old adversaries from the West Brom Vs Coventry derby games - remember during my days a sending-off was a rare occurrence and a stigma on the profession. I would like to put the records straight and categorically state that I was never sent-off during the whole of my playing career!"

....

PETER CRAIGMYLE (Referee) (An extract from 'Lifetime of Soccer')

"To referee a Scotland-England international at Hampden - that was one honour I cherished above all. For many, many years after I'd made a name for myself in the game, it seemed that this was going to be something I'd never achieve. At last - in 1941 - I was given the honour, and before I retired I'd been give it three times.

"They were all memorable games. But for me the one that sticks out like a sore thumb was my second, in 1943. In spite of the weather, I trained hard as usual every day in Pittodrie. On the Thursday before the big game I felt as fit as a fiddle, doing a few laps with some of the Aberdeen players. But at night I didn't feel so good - and on Friday morning it was painfully obvious that I was far from well. I phoned for the doctor - and got the shock of my life when he said: 'You must stay in bed for a least a few days. And, of course, you'll have to call-off the game tomorrow.'

"Call it off! Gosh, I'd rather risk my life! And that's just what I did. I told the doctor I'd call it off all right - just to put his mind at ease! - and immediately phoned my old friend George Anderson, Dundee director-manager, and asked him to come and see me. George phoned S.F.A. Secretary George Graham and told him the position. Said my 'chief - 'Tell Peter that if it's humanly possible, we want him to do the game.'

"That was enough for me. George and I agreed to 'kid' the doctor that I'd cancelled the appointment, and we planned a way of 'smuggling' me out of Aberdeen. And so, at 5.30 a.m. on the morning of the game, George called for me in his car and took me down to the station. What a morning! I staggered into the train, more dead than alive. With a pocketful of aspirins and a bottle of Scotch, I lay down the full length of a seat and a long nightmare journey to Glasgow began. By the time I arrived, there were a few aspirins and very little Scotch left!

"Well, the first half went over without a hitch. A pick-me-up at the interval and out I went again for that last 45 minutes of torture. Only with the utmost effort could I drag one leg after the other. And then it was all over and I was back in my dressing room.

"I'd only been back in my dressing-room a few minutes when everything became a complete blank - I fainted. I'd won my own personal battle against ill-health to referee that great game, but the battle for recovery was only beginning. I was brought round, thanked by the officials, and rushed off to the station. Then came another shock - the only train available was one that went the long route by Dundee, and even then, there wasn't a seat to be had. They stretched me out in the guard's van. A sorry, miserable figure I must have looked!

"My doctor was waiting for me at Aberdeen station. What he said is unprintable! And then he added: 'Aye, man, for the next six months you'll know all about it.' I did! In fact, I thought that I was finished with refereeing for good. But with a long holiday I fought back to health and strength again. Since then, I've often wondered whether anybody else has ever refereed with a temperature of 101."

Other books on the subject of British International players and matches

Although now out of print, a few copies of the following are still available
(April 1995), at the original cover prices)

"An English Football Internationalists' Who's Who 1872 - 1988"
By Douglas Lamming
300 pages, fully illustrated .... £9-50 plus £2-00 U.K. P/P.

"A Scottish Soccer Internationalists' Who's Who 1872 - 1986"
By Douglas Lamming
272 pages, fully illustrated .... £5-95 plus £2-00 U.K. P/P.

"Who's Who Of Welsh International Soccer Players 1876 - 1991"
By Gareth Davies & Ian Garland
240 large pages fully illustrated .... £16-95 plus £3-50 P/P.

----- **Special Offer** - All Three for £36-90 Including P/P. -----

Signed Limited Edition Print (only 50 produced, few left) of Johnny Mapson, the
Reading, Sunderland and England goalkeeper (as featured in the "Reminiscences"
illustration) .... Only £6-00 plus 50p P/P.

WANTED: Programmes of any 1939-46 matches involving the Scotland, Wales
or Northern Ireland international teams (except those Vs. England). Also match
action, pre-match presentations or team groups from any of the 1919 Victory and
1939-46 internationals for inclusion in the (provisional) follow-up volume
covering the Scottish Welsh and Irish wartime international players and matches.

All the above, please reply/make cheques payable to:
Beejay Soccer Enterprises, 275 Overdown Road, Tilehurst, Reading, RG31 6NX.

ALSO:

A concise and inexpensive reference booklet entitled *"International Line-ups and
Statistics - England 1872 - 1960".* Published (Soccer Book Publishing) April
1995. 52 page booklet includes the line-ups for every England full international
during the period (plus several photo's.) Price £5-95 plus 50p U.K. P/P.

Direct from:
Yore Publications, 12 The Furrows, Harefield, Middx., UB9 6AT.

Please Turn Over for other (more general) Football books

From
'YORE PUBLICATIONS'
12 The Furrows, Harefield,
Middx. UB9 6AT

(Free lists issued 3 times per year. For your first list please send a S.A.E.)

THE BRISTOL BABE - The First 100 Years of Bristol City(David Woods) A truly complete History, by the Club's foremost Historian. 320 near A4 size pages, packed with statistical facts (from the Southville and Bedminster days - complete statistics, incl. line-ups from 1887), features on the programmes, the Grounds, etc. Seasonal Reserve team summaries, comprehensive Who's Who section, and well illustrated. Hardback, Price £17-95 plus £3-75 postage

BREATHE ON 'EM SALOP - The Official History of Shrewsbury Town (Mike Jones) Written by local broadcaster and supporter, and includes detailed match statistics from 1886 with full line-ups from 1945. Well illustrated with substantial text section, 'one-liner' (Football League) Who's Who section, etc. 256 large page hardback. Excellent value at £14-95 plus £3-50 postage.

SOUTHEND UNITED - The Official History **(Reprint update to end of 1993/94 season)** *(Peter Mason)* An excellent read, by journalist and supporter Peter Mason, with detailed statistics, well illustraed, sections on supporters club, grounds, Who's Who, etc. (While stocks last) £17-95 plus £3-75 postage

DONNY - The Official History of Doncaster Rovers(Tony Bluff and Barry Watson) Statistics (1879 to 1993), line-ups (from 1901), well illustrated, plus full written history etc. 240 page hardback, Price £14-95 plus £1-80 postage.

COLCHESTER UNITED - The Official History of the 'U's' (Hal Mason) Former journalist and programme editor, relates this complete history of the Club since its formation in 1937 up to 1937 (including complete statistics and lineups). Large Hardback with dustjacket, 240 pages, priced £14-95 plus £2-70 postage.

AMBER IN THE BLOOD - History of Newport County: (Tony Ambrosen). The full story of football in Newport from the pre-County days up to 1993, and including Newport AFC. 176 large pages, statistics (seasonal appearances summary), well illustrated, Who's Who, etc. £13-95 plus £2-70 postage.

KILLIE - The Official History (125 Years of Kilmarnock F.C.) (David Ross). A very detailed history of Scotland's oldest professional Club. The statistics section (including line-ups) cover the period 1873 to 1994, and over 200 illustrations, incl.a team group for most seasons. A large hardback of 256 pages, priced £15-95 plus £3-50 postage.

REJECTED F.C. VOLUMES 1, 2 & 3 (Reprint) (By Dave Twydell) The revised editions of these popular books - now in hardback - comprehensive histories of ex-League clubs: Aberdare Athletic, Ashington, Bootle, Bradford (Park Avenue), Burton (Swifts, Wanderers and United), Gateshead/South Shields, Glossop, Loughborough, Nelson, Stalybridge Celtic and Workington (Vol. 1); Accrington/Accrington Stanley, Barrow, Darwen, Merthyr Town, Thames Association and (new addition) Leeds City (Vol. 2); Durham City, Gainsborough Trinity, Middlesbrough Ironopolis, New Brighton/New Brighton Tower, Northwich Victoria, Southport (plus new addition) Wigan Borough. Also contain the basic statistical details of each club. Volume 1 contains 288 well illustrated pages. (Volumes 2 and 3, similar format, each approx. 240 pages and available from June 1995). Each volume price £12-95 plus £1-30 postage. (Also *Rejected F.C. of Scotland:* Vol. 1 covers Edinburgh and The South (Edinburgh City, Leith Athletic, St.Bernards, Armadale, Broxburn United, Bathgate, Peebles Rovers, Mid-Annandale, Nithsdale Wanderers and Solway Star - 288 pages). Vol. 2 covers Glasgow and District (Abercorn, Arthurlie, Beith, Cambuslang, Clydebank, Cowlairs, Johnstone, Linthouse, Northern, Third Lanark, and Thistle - 240 pages). Each £12-95 plus £1-30 postage.

FOOTBALL LEAGUE - GROUNDS FOR A CHANGE (By Dave Twydell). A 424 page, A5 sized, Hardback book. A comprehensive study of all the Grounds on which the current English Football League clubs previously played. Every Club that has moved Grounds is included, with a 'Potted' history of each, plus 250 illustrations. Plenty of 'reading' material, as well as an interesting reference book. £13-95 Plus £1-70 Postage.

COVENTRY CITY WHO'S WHO (1908 - 1993) Martin and Paul O'Connor. 224 page hardback, a comprehensive Who's Who (Biographies, other clubs, statistics, etc.) Price £13-95 plus £1-70 postage (FEW ONLY LEFT)

WHOS' WHO OF LINCOLN CITY (1892 - 1994) Donald and Ian Nannestad. 190 large page soft covered book, includes brief history of club, well illustrated, etc. Excellent value at only £9-95 plus £1-20 postage.